MY RELIGION
– WHAT I BELIEVE

MY RELIGION
– WHAT I BELIEVE
BY
LEO TOLSTOY

My Religion – What I Believe

White Crow Books is an imprint of
White Crow Productions Ltd
PO Box 1013
Guildford
GU1 9EJ

www.whitecrowbooks.com

Text design and eBook production by Essential Works
www.essentialworks.co.uk

ISBN 978-1-907355-23-3
eBook ISBN 978-1-907355-70-7

Religion & Spirituality

Distributed in the UK by
Lightning Source Ltd.
Chapter House
Pitfield
Kiln Farm
Milton Keynes MK11 3LW

Distributed in the USA by
Lightning Source Inc.
246 Heil Quaker Boulevard
LaVergne
Tennessee 37086

Contents

Translator's Preface

To one not familiar with the Russian language the accessible data relative to the external life of Leo Nikolaevich Tolstoy, the author of this book, are, to say the least, not voluminous. His name does not appear in that heterogeneous record of celebrities known as *The Men of the Time*, nor is it to be found in M. Vapereau's comprehensive *Dictionnaire des Contemporains*. And yet Count Leo Tolstoy is acknowledged by competent critics to be a man of extraordinary genius, who, certainly in one instance, has produced a masterpiece of literature which will continue to rank with the great artistic productions of this age.

Perhaps it is enough for us to know that he was born on his father's estate in the Russian province of Tula, in the year 1828; that he received a good home education and studied the oriental languages at the University of Kasan that he was for a time in the army, which he entered at the age of twenty-three as an officer of artillery, serving later on the staff of Prince Gortschakof; and that subsequently he alternated between St. Petersburg and Moscow, leading the existence of super-refined barbarism and excessive luxury, characteristic of the Russian aristocracy. He saw life in country and city, in camp and court. He was numbered among the defenders of Sebastopol in the Crimean War and the impressions then gathered he used as material for a series of *War Sketches* that attracted attention in the pages of the magazine where they first appeared; and when, a little later, they were published in book form, their author, then twenty-eight years of age, acquired at once a wide popularity. Popularity became fame with the publication, also in 1856, of *Childhood and Youth*, remarkable alike for its artless revelations concerning the genesis and growth of ideas and emotions in the minds of the young, for its idyllic pictures of domestic life, and for its graceful descriptions of nature. This was followed by *The Cossacks*, a wild romance of the steppes, vigorously realistic in details, and, like all of Count Tolstoy's works, poetic in conception and inspired with a dramatic intensity. In

1860 appeared *War and Peace*, a historical romance in many volumes, dealing with the Napoleonic invasion of 1812 and the events that immediately followed the retreat from Moscow. According to M. C. Courriere, it was seized upon with avidity and produced a profound sensation.

"The stage is immense and the actors are innumerable; among them three emperors with their ministers, their marshals, and their generals, and then a countless retinue of minor officers, soldiers, nobles, and peasants.

We are transported by turns from the salons of St. Petersburg to the camps of war, from Moscow to the country. And all these diverse and varied scenes are joined together with a controlling purpose that brings everything into harmony. Each one of the prolonged series of constantly changing tableaux is of remarkable beauty and palpitating with life."

Pierre Besushkof, one of the three heroes of *War and Peace*, has, rightly or wrongly, long been regarded as in some respects an autobiographical study, but the personal note is always clearly perceptible in Count Tolstoy's writings, if we are to believe the reports of the enthusiastic purveyors of literary information who have made known some of their many attractive qualities. It is plain also that a common purpose runs through them all, a purpose which only in the author's latest production finds full expression. There are hints of it in *Childhood and Youth*; in *War and Peace*, and in a subsequent romance, *Anna Karenin*, it becomes very distinct. In the two works last named Count Tolstoy is pitiless in his portrayal of the vices and follies of the wealthy, aristocratic class, and warm in his praise of simplicity and unpretending virtue. Pierre Besushkof is represented as the product of a transition period, one who sees clearly that the future must be different from the past, but unable to interpret the prophecies of its coming. M. Courriere speaks of him very happily as "an overgrown child who seems to be lost in a wholly unfamiliar world."

For a time Pierre finds mental tranquillity in the tenets of freemasonry, and the author gives us a vivid account, humorous and pathetic by turns, of the young man's efforts to carry the newly acquired doctrines into practice. He determines to better the condition of the peasants on his estates; but instead of looking after the affair himself, he leaves the consummation of his plans to his stewards, with the result that "the cleverest among them listened with attention, but considered one thing only, how to carry out their own private ends under the pretence of executing his commands." Later on we are shown Pierre wandering aimlessly about the streets of burning Moscow, until taken into custody by the French. Then he learns the true meaning of life from a simple soldier, a fellow prisoner, and thereby realizes that safety for the future is to be obtained only by bringing life to the standard of rude simplicity adopted by the common people, by recognizing, in act as well as in deed, the brotherhood of man.

We cannot here enter into the question as to whether this mental attitude, by no means unusual among Russians of cultivation and liberality, arises from the lack of social gradation between the noble and the peasant, which forces the social philosopher of rank to accept an existence of pure worldliness and empty show, or to adopt the primitive aspirations and humble toil of the tillers of the soil. At any rate, it is plain that Count Tolstoy sides with the latter. The doctrine of simplification has many adherents in Russia, and when, some time ago, it was announced that the author of *War and Peace* had retired to the country and was leading a life of frugality and unaffected toil in the cultivation of his estates, the surprise to his own countrymen could not have been very great. In this book he tells us how the decision was formed. He bases his conclusions on a direct and literal interpretation of the teachings of Jesus as expressed in the Sermon on the Mount.

The interpretation is not new in theory, but never before has it been carried out with so much zeal, so much determination, so much sincerity, and, granting the premises, with logic so unanswerable, as in this beautiful confession of faith. How movingly does he depict the doubts and fears of the searcher after the better life; how impressive his earnest inquiry for truth; how inspiring his confidence in the natural goodness, as opposed to the natural depravity of man; how convincing his argument that the doctrine of Jesus is simple, practicable, and conducive to the highest happiness; how terrifying his enumeration of the sufferings of "the martyrs to the doctrine of the world"; how pitiless his arraignment of the Church for its complacent indifference to the welfare of humanity here in this present stage of existence; how sublime his prophecy of the golden age when men shall dwell together in the bonds of love, and sin and suffering shall be no more the common lot of mankind ! We read, and are thrilled with a divine emotion; but which of us is willing to accept the truth here unfolded as the veritable secret of life?

Shall we take seriously this eloquent enunciation of faith in humility, in self-denial, in fraternal love, or shall we regard it only as a beautiful and peaceful phase in the career of a man of genius who, after the storm and stress of a life of sin and suffering, has turned back to the ideals of youth and innocence, and sought to make them once more the objects of desire? Fanaticism, do you say? Ah, yes; but did not Jesus and his disciples practise just such fanaticism as this? Does anyone deny that all that is best in this modern world (and there is so much of the best, after all), that all that is best has come from the great moral impulse generated by a little group of fanatics in an obscure corner of Asia eighteen centuries ago? That impulse we still feel, in spite of all the obstructions that have been put in its way to nullify its action; and if any would seek for strength from the primary source of power, who shall say him nay? And so although we may smile at the artlessness of this Russian evangelist in his determination to find in the gospels the categorical imperative of self-renunciation, although we may regard with wonder the magnificent audacity of his exegetical speculations, we cannot refuse to admire a faith so sincere, so intense, and, in many respects, so elevating and so noble.

HUNTINGTON SMITH

Introduction

I HAVE NOT ALWAYS BEEN possessed of the religious ideas set forth in this book. For thirty-five years of my life I was, in the proper acceptation of the word, a nihilist, not a revolutionary socialist, but a man who believed in nothing. Five years ago faith came to me; I believed in the doctrine of Jesus, and my whole life underwent a sudden transformation. What I had once wished for I wished for no longer, and I began to desire what I had never desired before. What had once appeared to me right now became wrong, and the wrong of the past I beheld as right. My condition was like that of a man who goes forth upon some errand, and having traversed a portion of the road, decides that the matter is of no importance, and turns back. What was at first on his right hand is now on his left, and what was at his left hand is now on his right; instead of going away from his abode, he desires to get back to it as soon as possible. My life and my desires were completely changed; good and evil interchanged meanings. Why so? Because I understood the doctrine of Jesus in a different way from that in which I had understood it before.

It is not my purpose to expound the doctrine of Jesus; I wish only to tell how it was that I came to understand what there is in this doctrine that is simple, clear, evident, indisputable; how I under stand that part of it which appeals to all men, and how this understanding refreshed my soul and gave me happiness and peace.

I do not intend to comment on the doctrine of Jesus; I desire only that all comment shall be forever done away with. The Christian sects have always maintained that all men, however unequal in education and intelligence, are equal before God; that divine truth is accessible to every one. Jesus has even declared it to be the will of God that what is concealed from the wise shall be revealed to the simple. Not every one is able to understand the mysteries of dogmatics, homiletics, liturgies, hermeneutics, apologetics; but every one is able and ought to understand what Jesus Christ said to the millions of simple and ignorant people who have lived, and who are living today. Now, the things that

Jesus said to simple people who could not avail themselves of the comments of Paul of Clement, of Chrysostom and of others, are just what I did not understand, and which, now that I have come to understand them, I wish to make plain to all. The thief on the cross believed in the Christ, and was saved. If the thief, instead of dying on the cross, had descended from it, and told all men of his belief in the Christ, would not the result have been of great good? Like the thief on the cross, I believe in the doctrine of Jesus, and this belief has made me whole. This is not a vain comparison, but a truthful expression of my spiritual condition; my soul, once filled with despair of life and fear of death, is now full of happiness and peace.

Like the thief, I knew that my past and present life was vile; I saw that the majority of men about me lived unworthy lives. I knew, like the thief, that I was wretched and suffering, that all those about me suffered and were wretched; and I saw before me nothing but death to save me from this condition. As the thief was nailed to his cross, so I was nailed to a life of suffering and evil by an incomprehensible power. And as the thief saw before him, after the sufferings of a foolish life, the horrible shadows of death, so I beheld the same vista opening before me.

In all this I felt that I was like the thief. There was, however, a difference in our conditions; he was about to die, and I – I still lived. The dying thief thought perhaps to find his salvation beyond the grave, while I had before me life and its mystery this side the grave. I understood nothing of this life; it seemed to me a frightful thing, and then – I understood the words of Jesus, and life and death ceased to be evil; instead of despair, I tasted joy and happiness that death could not take away.

Will anyone, then, be offended if I tell the story of how all this came about?

LEO TOLSTOY
MOSCOW, JANUARY 22, 1884

Chapter 1

I SHALL EXPLAIN ELSEWHERE, in two voluminous treatises, why I did not understand the doctrine of Jesus, and how at length it became clear to me. These works are a criticism of dogmatic theology and a new translation of the four Gospels, followed by a concordance. In these writings I seek methodically to disentangle everything that tends to conceal the truth from men; I translate the four Gospels anew, verse by verse, and I bring them together in a new concordance. The work has lasted for six years. Each year, each month, I discover new meanings which corroborate the fundamental idea; I correct the errors which have crept in, and I put the last touches to what I have already written. My life, whose final term is not far distant, will doubtless end before I have finished my work; but I am convinced that the work will be of great service; so I shall do all that I can to bring it to completion.

I do not now concern myself with this outward work upon theology and the Gospels, but with an inner work of an entirely different nature. I have to do now with nothing systematic or methodical, only with that sudden light which showed me the Gospel doctrine in all its simple beauty.

The process was something similar to that experienced by one who, following an erroneous model, seeks to restore a statue from broken bits of marble, and who with one of the most refractory fragments in hand perceives the hopelessness of his ideal; then he begins anew, and instead of the former incongruities he finds, as he observes the outlines of each fragment, that all fit well together and form one consistent whole. That is exactly what happened to me, and is what I wish to relate. I wish to tell how I found the key to the true meaning of the doctrine of Jesus, and how by this meaning doubt was absolutely driven from my soul. The discovery came about in this way.

From my childhood, from the time I first began to read the New Testament, I was touched most of all by that portion of the doctrine of Jesus which inculcates love, humility, self-denial, and the duty of returning good for evil. This, to me, has always been the substance of Christianity; my heart recognized its truth in spite of scepticism and despair, and for this reason I submitted to a religion professed by a multitude of toilers, who find in it the solution of life, the religion taught by the Orthodox Church. But in making my submission to the Church, I soon saw that I should not find in its creed the confirmation of the essence of Christianity; what was to me essential seemed to be in the dogma of the Church merely an accessory. What was to me the most important of the teaching of Jesus was not so regarded by the Church. No doubt (I thought) the Church sees in Christianity, aside from its inner meaning of love, humility, and self-denial, an outer, dogmatic meaning, which, however strange and even repulsive to me, is not in itself evil or pernicious. But the further I went on in submission to the doctrine of the Church, the more clearly I saw in this particular point something of greater importance than I had at first realized. What I found most repulsive in the doctrine of the Church was the strangeness of its dogmas and the approval, nay, the support, which it gave to persecutions, to the death penalty, to wars stirred up by the intolerance common to all sects; but my faith was chiefly shattered by the indifference of the Church to what seemed to me essential in the teachings of Jesus, and by its avidity for what seemed to me of secondary importance. I felt that something was wrong; but I could not see where the fault lay, because the doctrine of the Church did not deny what seemed to me essential in the doctrine of Jesus; this essential was fully recognized, yet in such a way as not to give it the first place. I could not accuse the Church of denying the essence of the doctrine of Jesus, but it was recognized in a way which did not satisfy me. The Church did not give me what I expected from her. I had passed from nihilism to the Church simply because I felt it to be impossible to live without religion, that is, without a knowledge of good and evil beyond the animal instincts. I hoped to find this knowledge in Christianity; but Christianity I then saw only as a vague spiritual tendency, from which it was impossible to deduce any clear and peremptory rules for the guidance of life. These I sought and these I demanded of the Church. The Church offered me rules which not only did not inculcate the practice of the Christian life, but which made such practice still more difficult. I could not become a disciple of the Church. An existence based upon Christian truth was to me indispensable, and the Church only offered me rules completely at variance with the truth that I loved. The rules of the Church touching articles of faith, dogmas, the observance of the sacrament, fasts, prayers, were not necessary to me, and did not seem to be based on Christian truth. Moreover, the rules of the Church weakened and sometimes destroyed the desire for Christian truth which alone gave meaning to my life.

I was troubled most that the miseries of humanity, the habit of judging one another, of passing judgment upon nations and religions, and the wars and massacres which resulted in consequence, all went on with the approbation of the Church. The doctrine of Jesus – judge not, be humble, forgive offences, deny self, love – this doctrine was extolled by the church in words, but at the same time the Church approved what was incompatible with the doctrine. Was it possible that the doctrine of Jesus admitted of such contradiction? I could not believe so.

Another astonishing thing about the Church was that the passages upon which it based affirmation of its dogmas were those which were most obscure. On the other hand, the passages from which came the moral laws were the most clear and precise. And yet the dogmas and the duties depending upon them were definitely formulated by the Church, while the recommendation to obey the moral law was put in the most vague and mystical terms. Was this the intention of Jesus? The Gospels alone could dissipate my doubts. I read them once and again.

Of all the other portions of the Gospels, the Sermon on the Mount always had for me an exceptional importance. I now read it more frequently than ever. Nowhere does Jesus speak with greater solemnity, nowhere does he propound moral rules more definitely and practically, nor do these rules in any other form awaken more readily an echo in the human heart; nowhere else does he address himself to a larger multitude of the common people. If there are any clear and precise Christian principles, one ought to find them here. I therefore sought the solution of my doubts in Matthew v., vi and vii comprising the Sermon on the Mount. These chapters I read very often, each time with the same emotional ardor, as I came to the verses which exhort the hearer to turn the other cheek, to give up his cloak, to be at peace with all the world, to love his enemies, but each time with the same disappointment. The divine words were not clear. They exhorted to a renunciation so absolute as to entirely stifle life as I understood it; to renounce everything, therefore, could not, it seemed to me, be essential to salvation. And the moment this ceased to be an absolute condition, clearness and precision were at an end.

I read not only the Sermon on the Mount; I read all the Gospels and all the theological commentaries on the Gospels. I was not satisfied with the declarations of the theologians that the Sermon on the Mount was only an indication of the degree of perfection to which man should aspire; that man, weighed down by sin, could not reach such an ideal; and that the salvation of humanity was in faith and prayer and grace. I could not admit the truth of these propositions. It seemed to me a strange thing that Jesus should propound rules so clear and admirable, addressed to the understanding of every one, and still realize man's inability to carry his doctrine into practice.

Then as I read these maxims I was permeated with the joyous assurance that I might that very hour, that very moment, begin to practise them. The burning desire I felt led me to the attempt, but the doctrine of the Church rang in my ears – *Man is weak, and to this he cannot attain*; my strength soon failed. On every side I heard," *You must believe and pray*"; but my wavering faith impeded prayer. Again I heard, "You must pray, and God will give you faith; this faith will inspire prayer, which in turn will invoke faith that will inspire more prayer, and so on, indefinitely." Reason and experience alike convinced me that such methods were useless. It seemed to me that the only true way was for me to try to follow the doctrine of Jesus.

And so, after all this fruitless search and careful meditation over all that had been written for and against the divinity of the doctrine of Jesus, after all this doubt and suffering, I came back face to face with the mysterious Gospel message. I could not find the meanings that others found, neither could I discover what I sought. It was only after I had rejected the interpretations of the wise critics and theologians, according to the words of Jesus,

"Except ye . . . become as little children, ye shall not enter into the kingdom of heaven" (Matt, xviii. 3) , it was only then that I suddenly understood what had been so meaningless before. I understood, not through exegetical fantasies or profound and ingenious textual combinations; I understood everything, because I put all commentaries out of my mind. This was the passage that gave me the key to the whole:

"Ye have heard that it hath been said. An eye for an eye, and a tooth for a tooth: But I say unto you, that ye resist not evil." (Matt. v. 38, 39.)

One day the exact and simple meaning of these words came to me; I understood that Jesus meant neither more nor less than what he said. What I saw was nothing new; only the veil that had hidden the truth from me fell away, and the truth was revealed in all its grandeur.

"Ye have heard that it hath been said, an eye for an eye, and a tooth for a tooth: But I say unto you, that ye resist not evil."

These words suddenly appeared to me as if I had never read them before. Always before, when I had read this passage, I had, singularly enough, allowed certain words to escape me, But I say unto you, that ye resist not evil." To me it had always been as if the words just quoted had never existed, or had never possessed a definite meaning. Later on, as I talked with many Christians familiar with the Gospel, I noticed frequently the same blindness with regard to these words. No one remembered them, and often in speaking of this passage, Christians took up the Gospel to see for themselves if the words were really there. Through a similar neglect of these words I had failed to understand the words that follow:

But whosoever shall smite thee on thy right cheek, turn to him the other also (Matt. v. 39).

Always these words had seemed to me to demand long-suffering and privation contrary to human nature. They touched me; I felt that it would be noble to follow them, but I also felt that I had not the strength to put them into practice. I said to myself, "If I turn the other cheek, I shall get another blow; if I give, all that I have will be taken away. Life would be an impossibility. Since life is given to me, why should I deprive myself of it?

Jesus cannot demand as much as that." Thus I reasoned, persuaded that Jesus, in exalting long-suffering and privation, made use of exaggerated terms lacking in clearness and precision; but when I understood the words "Resist not evil" I saw that Jesus did not exaggerate, that he did not demand suffering for suffering, but that he had formulated with great clearness and precision exactly what he wished to say. *"Resist not evil,"* knowing that you will meet with those who, when they have struck you on one cheek and met with no resistance, will strike you on the other; who, having taken away your coat, will take away your cloak also; who, having profited by your labour, will force you to labour still more without reward. And yet, though all this should happen to you, "Resist not evil"; do good to them that injure you. When I understood these words as they are written, all that had been obscure became clear to me, and what had seemed exaggerated I saw to be perfectly reasonable. For the first time I grasped the pivotal idea in the words "Resist not evil"; I saw that what followed was only a development of this command; I saw that Jesus did not exhort us to turn the other cheek that we might endure suffering, but that his exhortation was, "Resist not evil" and that he afterward declared suffering to be the possible consequence of the practice of this maxim.

A father, when his son is about to set out on a far journey, commands him not to tarry by the way; he does not tell him to pass his nights without shelter, to deprive himself of food, to expose himself to rain and cold. He says, *"Go thy way, and tarry not, though thou shouldest be wet or cold."* So Jesus does not say, "Turn the other cheek and suffer." He says, "Resist not evil"; no matter what happens, "Resist not."

These words, "Resist not evil" when I under stood their significance, were to me the key that opened all the rest. Then I was astonished that I had failed to comprehend words so clear and precise.

"Ye have heard that it hath been said. An eye for an eye, and a tooth for a tooth: But I say unto you, that ye resist not evil."

Whatever injury the evil-disposed may inflict upon you, bear it, give all that you have, but resist not. Could anything be more clear, more definite, more intelligible than that? I had only to grasp the simple and exact meaning of these words, just as they were spoken, when the whole doctrine of Jesus, not only as set forth in the Sermon on the Mount, but in the entire Gospels, became clear to me; what had seemed contradictory was now in harmony; above all, what had seemed superfluous was now indispensable. Each portion fell into harmonious unison and filled its proper part, like the fragments of a broken statue when adjusted in harmony with the sculptor's design. In the Sermon on the Mount, as well as throughout the whole Gospel, I found everywhere affirmation of the same doctrine, "Resist not evil"

In the Sermon on the Mount, as well as in many other places, Jesus represents his disciples, those who observe the rule of non-resistance to evil, as turning the other cheek, giving up their cloaks, persecuted, used despitefully, and in want. Everywhere Jesus says that he who taketh not up his cross, he who does not renounce worldly advantage, he who is not ready to bear all the consequences of the commandment, "Resist not evil" cannot become his disciple.

To his disciples Jesus says, Choose to be poor; bear all things without resistance to evil, even though you thereby bring upon yourself persecution, suffering, and death.

Prepared to suffer death rather than resist evil, he reproved the resentment of Peter, and died exhorting his followers not to resist and to remain always faithful to his doctrine. The early disciples observed this rule, and passed their lives in misery and persecution, without rendering evil for evil.

It seems, then, that Jesus meant precisely what he said. We may declare the practice of such a rule to be very difficult; we may deny that he who follows it will find happiness; we may say with the unbelievers that Jesus was a dreamer, an idealist who propounded impracticable maxims; but it is impossible not to admit that he expressed in a manner at once clear and precise what he wished to say; that is, that according to his doctrine a man must not resist evil, and, consequently, that whoever adopts his doctrine will not resist evil. And yet neither believers nor unbelievers will admit this simple and clear interpretation of Jesus' words.

Chapter 2

WHEN I APPREHENDED clearly the words "Resist not evil" my conception of the doctrine of Jesus was entirely changed; and I was astounded, not that I had failed to understand it before, but that I had misunderstood it so strangely. I knew, as we all know, that the true significance of the doctrine of Jesus was comprised in the injunction to love one's neighbor. When we say, "Turn the other cheek" "Love your enemies," we express the very essence of Christianity. I knew all that from my childhood; but why had I failed to understand aright these simple words? Why had I always sought for some ulterior meaning? Resist not evil" means, never resist, never oppose violence; or, in other words, never do anything contrary to the law of love. If anyone takes advantage of this disposition and affronts you, bear the affront, and do not, above all, have recourse to violence. This Jesus said in words so clear and simple that it would be impossible to express the idea more clearly. How was it then, that believing or trying to believe these to be the words of God, I still maintained the impossibility of obeying them? If my master says to me, "Go; cut some wood," and I reply, "It is beyond my strength," I say one of two things: either I do not believe what my master says, or I do not wish to obey his commands. Should I then say of God's commandment that I could not obey it without the aid of a supernatural power? Should I say this without having made the slightest effort of my own to obey? We are told that God descended to earth to save mankind; that salvation was secured by the second person of the Trinity, who suffered for men, thereby redeeming them from sin, and gave them the Church as the shrine for the transmission of grace to all believers; but aside from this, the Saviour gave to men a doctrine and the example of his own life for their salvation. How, then, could I say that the rules of life which Jesus has formulated so clearly and simply for every one how could I say that these rules were difficult to obey, that it was impossible to obey them without the assistance of a supernatural power? Jesus saw no such impossibility; he distinctly declared that those who did not obey could not enter into the kingdom of God. Nowhere did he say that obedience would be difficult; on the contrary, he said in so many words, "My yoke is easy and my burden is light" (Matt. xi. 30). And John, the evangelist, says, "His commandments are not grievous" (I John v. 3). Since God declared the practice of his law to be easy, and himself practised it in human form, as did also his disciples, how dared I speak of the impossibility of obedience without the aid of a supernatural power?

If one bent all his energies to overthrow any law, what could he say of greater force than that the law was essentially impracticable, and that the maker of the law knew it to be impracticable and unattainable without the aid of a supernatural power? Yet that is exactly what I had been thinking of the command, "Resist not evil." I endeavored to find out how it was that I got the idea that Jesus law was divine, but that it could not be obeyed; and as I reviewed my past history, I perceived that the idea had not been communicated to me in all its crudeness (it would then have been revolting to me), but insensibly I had been imbued with it from childhood, and all my after life had only confirmed me in error. From my childhood I had been taught that Jesus was God, and that his doctrine was divine, but at the same time I was taught to respect as sacred the institutions which protected me from violence and evil. I was taught to resist evil, that it was humiliating to submit to evil, and that resistance to it was praiseworthy. I was taught to judge, and to inflict punishment. Then I was taught the soldier's trade, that is, to resist evil by homicide; the army to which I belonged was called "The Christophile Army," and it was sent forth with a Christian benediction. From infancy to manhood I learned to venerate things that were in direct contradiction to the law of Jesus, to meet an aggressor with his own weapons, to avenge myself by violence for all offences against my person, my family, or my race. Not only was I not blamed for this; I learned to regard it as not at all contrary to the law of Jesus. All that surrounded me, my personal security and that of my family and my property depended then upon a law which Jesus reproved, the law of "a tooth for a tooth." My spiritual instructors taught me that the law of Jesus was divine, but, because of human weakness, impossible of practice, and that the grace of Jesus

Christ alone could aid us to follow its precepts. And this instruction agreed with what I received in secular institutions and from the social organization about me. I was so thoroughly possessed with this idea of the impracticability of the divine doctrine; the idea conformed so well with my desires, that not till the time of awakening, I realize its falsity. I did not see how impossible it was to confess Jesus and his doctrine, "Resist not evil" and at the same time deliberately assist in the organization of property, of tribunals, of governments, of armies; to contribute to the establishment of a polity entirely contrary to the doctrine of Jesus, and at the same time pray to Jesus to help us to obey his commands, to forgive our sins, and to aid us that we resist not evil. I did not see, what is very clear to me now, how much more simple it would be to organize a method of living conformable to the law of Jesus, and then to pray for tribunals, and massacres, and wars, if these things were indispensable to our happiness.

Thus I came to understand the source of error into which I had fallen. I had confessed Jesus with my lips, but my heart was still far from him. The command, "Resist not evil" is the central point of Jesus doctrine; it is not a mere verbal affirmation; it is a rule whose practice is obligatory. It is verily the key to the whole mystery; but the key must be thrust to the bottom of the lock. When we regard it as a command impossible of performance, the value of the entire doctrine is lost. Why should not a doctrine seem impracticable, when we have suppressed its fundamental proposition? It is not strange that unbelievers look upon it as totally absurd. When we declare that one may be a Christian without observing the commandment, "Resist not evil," we simply leave out the connecting link which transmits the force of the doctrine of Jesus into action.

Some time ago I was reading in Hebrew, the fifth chapter of Matthew with a Jewish rabbi. At nearly every verse the rabbi said, "This is in the Bible," or "This is in the Talmud," and he showed me in the Bible and in the Talmud sentences very like the declarations of the Sermon on the Mount. When we reached the words, "Resist not evil," the rabbi did not say, "This is in the Talmud," but he asked me, with a smile, "Do the Christians obey this command? Do they turn the other cheek?" I had nothing to say in reply, especially as at that particular time, Christians, far from turning the other cheek, were smiting the Jews upon both cheeks. I asked him if there were anything similar in the Bible or in the Talmud. "No," he replied, "there is nothing like it; but tell me, do the Christians obey this law?" It was only another way of saying that the presence in the Christian doctrine of a commandment which no one observed, and which Christians themselves regarded as impracticable, is simply an avowal of the foolishness and nullity of that law. I could say nothing in reply to the rabbi.

Now that I understand the exact meaning of the doctrine, I see clearly the strangely contradictory position in which I was placed. Having recognized the divinity of Jesus and of his doctrine, and having at the same time organized a life wholly contrary to that doctrine, what remained for me but to look upon the doctrine as impracticable? In words I had recognized the doctrine of Jesus as sacred; in actions, I had professed a doctrine not at all Christian, and I had recognized and reverenced the anti-Christian customs which hampered my life upon every side. The persistent message of the Old Testament is that misfortunes came upon the Hebrew people because they believed in false gods and denied Jehovah. Samuel (I. viii–xii.) accuses the people of adding to their other apostasies the choice of a man, upon whom they depended for deliverance instead of upon Jehovah, who was their true King. "Turn not aside after vain things," Samuel says to the people (I. xii. 21); "turn not aside after vain things, which cannot profit nor deliver; for they are vain." Fear Jehovah and serve him. But if ye shall still do wickedly, ye shall be consumed, both ye and your king" (I. xii. 24, 25). And so with me, faith in *tohu*, in vain things, in empty idols, had concealed the truth from me. Across the path which led to the truth, thou, the idol of vain things, rose before me, cutting off the light, and I had not the strength to beat it down.

On a certain day, at this time, I was walking in Moscow towards the Borovitzky Gate, where was stationed an old lame beggar, with a dirty cloth wrapped about his head. I took out my purse to bestow alms; but at the same moment I saw a young soldier emerging from the Kremlin at a rapid pace, head well up, red of face, wearing the State insignia of military dignity. The beggar, on perceiving the soldier, arose in fear, and ran with all his might towards the Alexander Garden. The soldier, after a vain attempt to come up with the fugitive, stopped, shouting forth an imprecation upon the poor wretch who had established himself under the gateway contrary to regulations. I waited for the soldier. When he approached me, I asked him if he knew how to read.

Yes. Why do you ask?"

"Have you read the New Testament?"

"Yes."

"And do you remember the words, if thine enemy hunger, feed him?"

I repeated the passage. He remembered it, and heard me to the end. I saw that he was uneasy. Two passersby stopped and listened. The soldier seemed to be troubled that he should be condemned for doing his duty in driving persons away from a place where they had been forbidden to linger. He thought himself at fault, and sought for an excuse.

Suddenly his eye brightened; he looked at me over his shoulder, as if he were about to move away.

"And the military regulation, do you know any thing about that?" he demanded.

"No," I said.

"In that case, you have nothing to say to me," he retorted, with a triumphant wag of the head, and elevating his plume once more, he marched away to his post. He was the only man that I ever met who had solved, with an inflexible logic, the question which eternally confronted me in social relations, and which rises continually before every man who calls himself a Christian.

Chapter 3

WE ARE WRONG WHEN we say that the Christian doctrine is concerned only with the salvation of the individual, and has nothing to do with questions of State. Such an assertion is simply a bold affirmation of an untruth, which, when we examine it seriously, falls of itself to the ground. It is well (so I said); I will resist not evil; I will turn the other cheek in private life; but hither comes the enemy, or here is an oppressed nation, and I am called upon to do my part in the struggle against evil, to go forth and kill. I must decide the question, to serve God or *tohu*, to go to war or not to go. Perhaps I am a peasant; I am appointed mayor of a village, a judge, a jury man; I am obliged to take the oath of office, to judge, to condemn. What ought I to do? Again I must choose between the divine law and the human law. Perhaps I am a monk living in a monastery; the neighboring peasants trespass upon our pasturage, and I am appointed to resist evil, to plead for justice against the wrongdoers. Again I must choose. It is a dilemma from which no man can escape.

I do not speak of those whose entire lives are passed in resisting evil, as military authorities, judges, or governors. No one is so obscure that he is not obliged to choose between the service of God and the service of *tohu*, in his relation to the State. My very existence, entangled with that of the State and the social existence organized by the State, exacts from me an anti-Christian activity directly contrary to the commandments of Jesus. In fact, with conscription and compulsory jury service, this pitiless dilemma arises before every one. Every one is forced to take up murderous weapons; and even if he does not get as far as murder, his weapons must be ready, his carbine loaded, and his sword keen of edge, that he may declare himself ready for murder. Every one is forced into the service of the courts to take part in meting out judgment and sentence; that is, to deny the commandment of Jesus, "Resist not evil," in acts as well as in words.

The soldier's problem, the Gospel or military regulations, divine law or human law, is before mankind today as it was in the time of Samuel. It was forced upon Jesus and upon his disciples; it is forced in these times upon all who would be Christians; and it was forced upon me.

The law of Jesus, with its doctrine of love, humility, and self-denial, touched my heart more deeply than ever before. But everywhere, in the annals of history, in the events that were going on about me, in my individual life, I saw the law opposed in a manner revolting to sentiment, conscience, and reason, and encouraging to brute instincts. I felt that if I adopted the law of Jesus, I should be alone; I should pass many unhappy hours; I should be persecuted and afflicted as Jesus had said. But if I adopted the human law, everybody would approve; I should be in peace and safety, with all the resources of civilization at my command to put my conscience at case. As Jesus said, I should laugh and be glad. I felt all this, and so I did not analyze the meaning of the doctrine of Jesus, but sought to understand it in such a way that it might not interfere with my life as an animal. That is, I did not wish to under stand it at all. This determination not to under stand led me into delusions which now astound me. As an instance in point, let me explain my former understanding of these words:

"Judge not, that ye be not judged." (Matt. vii. 1.) "Judge not, and ye shall not be judged; condemn not, and ye shall not be condemned." (Luke vi. 37.) The courts in which I served, and which insured the safety of my property and my person, seemed to be institutions so indubitably sacred and so entirely in accord with the divine law, it had never entered into my head that the words I have quoted could have any other meaning than an injunction not to speak ill of one's neighbor. It never occurred to me that Jesus spoke in these words of the courts of human law and justice. It was only when I under stood the true meaning of the words, "Resist not evil," that the question arose as to Jesus advice with regard to tribunals. When I understood that Jesus would denounce them, I asked myself, Is not this the real meaning: Not only do not judge your neighbor, do not speak ill of him, but do not judge him in the courts, do not judge him in any of the tribunals that you have instituted? Now in Luke (vi. 07–19) these words follow immediately the doctrine that exhorts us to resist not evil and to do good to our enemies. And after the injunction,

"Be ye therefore merciful, as your Father also is merciful," Jesus says, "Judge not, and ye shall not be judged; condemn not, and ye shall not be condemned." "Judge not;" does not this mean, Institute no tribunals for the judgment of your neighbor? I had only to bring this boldly before myself when heart and reason united in an affirmative reply.

To show how far I was before from the true interpretation, I shall confess a foolish pleasantry for which I still blush. When I was reading the New Testament as a divine book at the time that I had become a believer, I was in the habit of saying to my friends who were judges or attorneys, "And you still judge, although it is said, Judge not, and ye shall not be judged?" I was so sure that these words could have no other meaning than a condemnation of evil speaking that I did not comprehend the horrible blasphemy which I thus committed. I was so thoroughly convinced that these words did not mean what they did mean, that I quoted them in their true sense in the form of a pleasantry.

I shall relate in detail how it was that all doubt with regard to the true meaning of these words was effaced from my mind, and how I saw their purport to be that Jesus denounced the institution of all human tribunals, of whatever sort; that he meant to say so, and could not have expressed himself otherwise. When I understood the command, "Resist not evil" in its proper sense, the first thing that occurred to me was that tribunals, instead of con forming to this law, were directly opposed to it, and indeed to the entire doctrine; and therefore that if Jesus had thought of tribunals at all, he would have condemned them.

Jesus said, *"Resist not evil"*; the sole aim of tribunals is to resist evil. Jesus exhorted us to return good for evil; tribunals return evil for evil. Jesus said that we were to make no distinction between those who do good and those who do evil; tribunals do nothing else. Jesus said, Forgive, forgive not once or seven times, but without limit; love your enemies, do good to them that hate you but tribunals do not forgive, they punish; they re turn not good but evil to those whom they regard as the enemies of society. It would seem, then, that Jesus denounced judicial institutions. Perhaps (I said) Jesus never had anything to do with courts of justice, and so did not think of them, but I saw that such a theory was not tenable. Jesus, from his childhood to his death, was concerned with the tribunals of Herod, of the Sanhedrim, and of the High Priests. I saw that Jesus must have regarded courts of justice as wrong. He told his disciples that they would be dragged before the judges, and gave them advice as to how they should comport themselves. He said of himself that he should be condemned by a tribunal, and he showed what the attitude toward judges ought to be. Jesus, then, must have thought of the judicial institutions which condemned him and his disciples; which have condemned and continue to condemn millions of men.

Jesus saw the wrong and faced it. When the sentence against the woman taken in adultery was about to be carried into execution, he absolutely denied the possibility of human justice, and demonstrated that man could not be the judge since man himself was guilty. And this idea he has propounded many times, as where it is declared that one with a beam in his eye cannot see the mote in another's eye, or that the blind cannot lead the blind. He even pointed out the consequences of such misconceptions; the disciple would be above his Master.

Perhaps, however, after having denounced the incompetency of human justice as displayed in the case of the woman taken in adultery, or illustrated in the parable of the mote and the beam; perhaps, after all, Jesus would admit of an appeal to the justice of men where it was necessary for protection against evil; but I soon saw that this was inadmissible. In the Sermon on the Mount, he says, addressing the multitude:

"And if any man will sue thee at the law, and take away thy coat, let him have thy cloak also." (Matt. v. 40.)

Once more, perhaps Jesus spoke only of the personal bearing which a man should have when brought before judicial institutions, and did not condemn justice, but admitted the necessity in a Christian society of individuals who judge others in properly constituted forms. But I saw that this view was also inadmissible. When he prayed, Jesus besought all men, without exception, to forgive others, that their own trespasses might be forgiven. This thought he often expresses. He who brings his gift to the altar with prayer must first grant forgiveness. How, then, could a man judge and condemn when his religion commanded him to for give all trespasses, without limit? So I saw that according to the doctrine of Jesus no Christian judge could pass sentence of condemnation.

But might not the relation between the words "Judge not, and ye shall not be judged" and the preceding or subsequent passages permit us to conclude that Jesus, in saying, "Judge not," had no reference whatever to judicial institutions? No; this could not be so; on the contrary, it is clear from the relation of the phrases that in saying, "Judge not," Jesus did actually speak of judicial institutions. According to Matthew and Luke, before saying "Judge not, condemn not," his command was to resist not evil. And prior to this, as Matthew tells us, he repeated the ancient criminal law of the Jews, "An eye for an eye, and a tooth for a tooth." Then, after this reference to the old criminal law, he added, "But I say unto you, that ye resist not evil"; and, after that, "Judge not." Jesus did, then, refer directly to human criminal law, and repudiated it in the words, "Judge not." Moreover, according to Luke, he not only said, "Judge not," but also, "Condemn not." It was not without purpose that he added this almost synonymous word; it shows clearly what meaning should be attributed to the other. If he had wished to say, "Judge not your neighbor," he would have said neighbor" but he added the words which are translated "Condemn not," and then completed the sentence, "And ye shall not be condemned: forgive, and ye shall be forgiven." But some may still insist that Jesus, in expressing himself in this way, did not refer at all to the tribunals, and that I have read my own thoughts into his teachings. Let the apostles tell us what they thought of courts of justice, and if they recognized and approved of them. The apostle James says (iv. 11, 12):

"Speak not evil one of another, brethren. He that speaketh evil of his brother, and judgeth his brother, speaketh evil of the law, and judgeth the law: but if thou judge the law, thou art not a doer of the law, but judge. There is one lawgiver, who is able to save and to destroy: who art thou that judges another "

The word translated "speak evil "is the verb καταλαλεω which means "to speak against, to accuse "; this is its true meaning, as anyone may find out for himself by opening a dictionary. In the translation we read, "He that speaketh evil of his brother, speaketh evil of the law." Why so? Is the question that involuntarily arises. I may speak evil of my brother, but I do not thereby speak evil of the law. If, however, I accuse my brother, if I bring him to justice, it is plain that I thereby accuse the law of Jesus of insufficient: I accuse and judge the law. It is clear, then, that I do not practice the law, but that I make myself a judge of the law. "Not to judge, but to save" is Jesus declaration. How then shall I, who cannot save, become a judge and punish? The entire passage refers to human justice, and denies its authority. The whole epistle is permeated with the same idea. In the second chapter we read:

"For he shall have judgment without mercy, that hath showed no mercy; and mercy is exalted above judgment." 1 (James ii. 13.)

(The last phrase has been translated in such a way as to declare that judgment is compatible with Christianity, but that it ought to be merciful.)

James exhorts his brethren to have no respect of persons. If you have respect of the condition of persons, you are guilty of sin; you are like the untrustworthy judges of the tribunals. You look upon the beggar as the refuse of society, while it is the rich man who ought to be so regarded. He it is who oppresses you and draws you before the judgment seats. If you live according to the law of love for your neighbor, according to the law of mercy (which James calls "the law of liberty" to distinguish it from all others) if you live according to this law, it is well. But if you have respect of her sons, you transgress the law of mercy. Then (doubtless thinking of the case of the woman taken in adultery, who, when she was brought before Jesus, was about to be put to death according to the law), thinking, no doubt, of that case, James says that he who inflicts death upon the adulterous woman would himself be guilty of murder, and thereby transgress the eternal law; for the same law forbids both adultery and murder.

"So speak ye, and so do, as they that shall be judged by the law of liberty. For he shall have judgment without mercy, that hath showed no mercy; and mercy is exalted above judgment." (James ii. 12, 13.)

Could the idea be expressed in terms more clear and precise? Discrimination of persons is forbidden, as well as any judgment that shall classify persons as good or bad; human judgment is declared to be inevitably defective, and such judgment is denounced as criminal when it condemns for crime; judgment is blotted out by the eternal law, the law of mercy.

I open the epistles of Paul, who had been a victim of tribunals, and in the letter to the Romans I read the admonitions of the apostle for the vices and errors of those to whom his words are addressed; among other matters he speaks of courts of justice:

"Who, knowing the judgment of God, that they which commit such things are worthy of death, not only do the same, but have pleasure in them that do them. (Rom. i. 32.)

"Wherefore thou art inexcusable, O man, whosoever thou art that judgest: for wherein thou judges another, thou condemnest thyself; for thou that judgest dost the same things. (Rom. ii. 1.)

"Or despisest thou the riches of his goodness and forbearance and long suffering, not knowing that the goodness of God leadeth thee to repentance?" (Rom.ii. 4.)

Such was the opinion of the apostles with regard to tribunals, and we know that human justice was among the trials and sufferings that they endured with steadfastness and resignation to the will of God. When we think of the situation of the early Christians, surrounded by unbelievers, we can under stand the futility of denying to tribunals the right to judge persecuted Christians. The apostles spoke casually of tribunals as grievous, and denied their authority on every occasion.

I examined the teachings of the early Fathers of the Church, and found them to agree in obliging no one to judge or to condemn, and in urging all to bear the inflictions of justice. The martyrs, by their acts, declared themselves to be of the same mind. I saw that Christianity before Constantine regarded tribunals only as an evil which was to be endured with patience; but it never could have occurred to any early Christian that he could take part in the administration of the courts of justice.

It is plain, therefore, that Jesus words, "Judge not, condemn not," were understood by his first disciples, as they ought to be understood now, in their direct and literal meaning: judge not in courts of justice; take no part in them.

All this seemed absolutely to corroborate my conviction that the words, "Judge not, condemn not," referred to the justice of tribunals. Yet the meaning, "Speak not evil of your neighbor," is so firmly established, and courts of justice flaunt their decrees with so much assurance and audacity in all Christian societies, with the support even of the Church, that for a long time still I doubted the wisdom of my interpretation. If men have understood the words in this way (I thought), and have instituted Christian tribunals, they must certainly have some reason for so doing; there must be a good reason for regarding these words as a denunciation of evil-speaking, and there is certainly a basis of some sort for the institution of Christian tribunals; perhaps, after all, I am in the wrong.

I turned to the Church commentaries. In all, from the fifth century onward, I found the invariable interpretation to be, "Accuse not your neighbor;" that is, avoid evil speaking. As the words came to be understood exclusively in this sense, a difficulty arose, How to refrain from judgment? It being impossible not to condemn evil, all the commentators discussed the question, what is blamable and what is not blamable? Some, such as Chrysostom and Theophylact, said that, as far as servants of the Church were concerned, the phrase could not be construed as a prohibition of censure, since the apostles themselves were censorious. Others said that Jesus doubtless referred to the Jews, who accused their neighbors of shortcomings, and were themselves guilty of great sins.

Nowhere a word about human institutions, about tribunals, to show how they were affected by the warning, "Judge not." Did Jesus sanction courts of justice, or did he not? To this very natural question I found no reply as if it was evident that from the moment a Christian took his seat on the judge's bench he might not only judge his neighbor, but condemn him to death.

I turned to other writers, Greek, Catholic, Protestant, to the Tubingen school, to the historical school. Everywhere, even by the most liberal commentators, the words in question were interpreted as an injunction against evil speaking.

But why, contrary to the spirit of the whole doctrine of Jesus, are these words interpreted in so narrow a way as to exclude courts of justice from the injunction, "Judge not"? Why the supposition that Jesus in forbidding the comparatively light offence of speaking evil of one's neighbor did not forbid, did not even consider, the more deliberate judgment which results in punishment inflicted upon the condemned? To all this I got no response; not even an allusion to the least possibility that the words "to judge" could be used as referring to a court of justice, to the tribunals from whose punishments so many millions have suffered.

Moreover, when the words, "Judge not, condemn not," are under discussion, the cruelty of judging in courts of justice is passed over in silence, or else commended. The commentators all declare that in Christian societies tribunals are necessary, and in no way contrary to the law of Jesus.

Realizing this, I began to doubt the sincerity of the commentators; and I did what I should have done in the first place; I turned to the textual translations of the words which we render "to judge" and "to condemn." In the original these words are κρινω and καταδικαζω. The defective translation in James of καταλαλεω, which is rendered "to speak evil," strengthened my doubts as to the correct translation of the others. When I looked through different versions of the Gospels, I found καταδικαζω rendered in the Vulgate by *condemnare*, "to condemn"; in the Slavonian text the rendering is equivalent to that of the Vulgate; Luther has *verdammen*, "To speak evil of." These divergent renderings increased my doubts, and I was obliged to ask again the meaning of κρινω, as used by the two evangelists, and of καταδικαζω as used by Luke who, scholars tell us, wrote very correct Greek.

How would these words be translated by a man who knew nothing of the evangelical creed, and who had before him only the phrases in which they are used? Consulting the dictionary, I found that the word κρινω had several different meanings, among the most used being "to condemn in a court of justice," and even "to condemn to death," but in no instance did it signify "to speak evil." I consulted a dictionary of New Testament Greek, and found that was often used in the sense "to condemn in a court of justice," sometimes in the sense "to choose," never as meaning "to speak evil." From which I inferred that the word κρινω might be translated in different ways, but that the rendering "to speak evil" was the most forced and far fetched.

I searched for the word καταδικαζω, which follows κρινω, evidently to define more closely the sense in which the latter is to be understood. I looked for καταδικαζω in the dictionary, and found that it had no other signification than "to condemn in judgment," or "to judge worthy of death." I found that the word was used four times in the New Testament, each time in the sense "to condemn under sentence, to judge worthy of death." In James (v. 6) we read, "Ye have condemned and killed the just." The word rendered "condemned" is this same καταδικαζω, and is used with reference to Jesus, who was condemned to death by a court of justice. The word is never used in any other sense, in the New Testament or in any other writing in the Greek language.

What, then, are we to say to all this? Is my conclusion a foolish one? Is not every one who considers the fate of humanity filled with horror at the sufferings inflicted upon mankind by the enforcement of criminal codes, a scourge to those who condemn as well as to the condemned, from the slaughters of Genghis Khan to those of the French Revolution and the executions of our own times? He would indeed be without compassion, who could refrain from feeling horror and repulsion, not only at the sight of human beings thus treated by their kind, but at the simple recital of death inflicted by the knout, the guillotine, or the gibbet.

The Gospel, of which every word is sacred to you, declares distinctly and without equivocation: "You have from of old a criminal law, An eye for an eye, a tooth for a tooth; but a new law is given you, That you resist not evil. Obey this law; render not evil for evil, but do good to everyone, forgive everyone, under all circumstances." Further on comes the injunction, "Judge not," and that these words might not be misunderstood, Jesus added, "Condemn not; condemn not in justice the crimes of others."

"No more death warrants," said an inner voice "no more death warrants," said the voice of science; "evil cannot suppress evil." The Word of God, in which I believed, told me the same thing. And when in reading the doctrine, I came to the words,

"Condemn not, and ye shall not be condemned: forgive, and ye shall be forgiven," could I look upon them as meaning simply that I was not to indulge in gossip and evil speaking, and should continue to regard tribunals as a Christian institution, and myself as a Christian judge?

I was overwhelmed with horror at the grossness of the error into which I had fallen.

Chapter 4

Now i understood the words of Jesus: "Ye have heard that it hath been said, an eye for an eye, and a tooth for a tooth: but I say unto you, that ye resist not evil." Jesus meaning is: "You have thought that you were acting in a reasonable manner in defending yourself by violence against evil, in tearing out an eye for an eye, by fighting against evil with criminal tribunals, guardians of the peace, armies; but I say unto you, Renounce violence; have nothing to do with violence; do harm to no one, not even to your enemy." I understood now that in saying "Resist not evil," Jesus not only told us what would result from the observance of this rule, but established a new basis for society conformable to his doctrine and opposed to the social basis established by the law of Moses, by Roman law, and by the different codes in force today. He formulated a new law whose effect would be to deliver humanity from its self-inflicted woes. His declaration was: "You believe that your laws reform criminals; as a matter of fact, they only make more criminals. There is only one way to suppress evil, and that is to return good for evil, without respect of persons. For thousands of years you have tried the other method; now try mine, try the reverse."

Strange to say, in these later days, I talked with different persons about this commandment of Jesus, "Resist not evil" and rarely found anyone to coincide with my opinion! Two classes of men would never, even by implication, admit the literal interpretation of the law. These men were at the extreme poles of the social scale; they were the conservative Christian patriots who maintained the infallibility of the Church, and the atheistic revolutionists. Neither of these two classes was willing to renounce the right to resist by violence what they regarded as evil. And the wisest and most intelligent among them would not acknowledge the simple and evident truth, that if we once admit the right of any man to resist by violence what he regards as evil, every other man has equally the right to resist by violence what he regards as evil.

Not long ago I had in my hands an interesting correspondence between an orthodox Slavophile and a Christian revolutionist. The one advocated violence as a partisan of a war for the relief of brother Slavs in bondage; the other, as a partisan of revolution, in the name of our brothers the oppressed Russian peasantry. Both invoked violence, and each based himself upon the doctrine of Jesus. The doctrine of Jesus is understood in a hundred different ways; but never, unhappily, in the simple and direct way which harmonizes with the inevitable meaning of Jesus words.

Our entire social fabric is founded upon principles that Jesus reproved; we do not wish to understand his doctrine in its simple and direct acceptation, and yet we assure ourselves and others that we follow his doctrine, or else that his doctrine is not expedient for us. Believers profess that Christ as God, the second person of the Trinity, descended upon earth to teach men by his example how to live; they go through the most elaborate ceremonies for the consummation of the sacraments, the building of temples, the sending out of missionaries, the establishment of priesthoods, for parochial administration, for the performance of rituals; but they forget one little detail, the practice of the commandments of Jesus. Unbelievers endeavor in every possible way to organize their existence independent of the doctrine of Jesus, they having decided a priori that this doctrine is of no account. But to endeavor to put his teachings in practice, this each refuses to do; and the worst of it is, that with out any attempt to put them in practice, both believers and unbelievers decide a priori that it is impossible.

Jesus said, simply and clearly, that the law of resistance to evil by violence, which has been made the basis of society, is false, and contrary to man's nature; and he gave another basis, that of non-resistance to evil, a law which, according to his doctrine, would deliver man from wrong. "You believe" (he says in substance) "that your laws, which resort to violence, correct evil; not at all; they only augment it. For thousands of years you have tried to destroy evil by evil, and you have not destroyed it; you have only augmented it. Do as I command you, follow my example, and you will know that my doctrine is true." Not only in words, but by his acts, by his death, did Jesus propound his doctrine, "Resist not evil."

Believers listen to all this. They hear it in their churches, persuaded that the words are divine; they worship Jesus as God, and then they say: "All this is admirable, but it is impossible; as society is now organized, it would derange our whole existence, and we should be obliged to give up the customs that are so dear to us. We believe it all, but only in this sense: That it is the ideal toward which humanity ought to move; the ideal which is to be attained by prayer, and by believing in the sacraments, in the redemption, and in the resurrection of the dead."

The others, the unbelievers, the free-thinkers who comment on the doctrine of Jesus, the historians of religions, the Strausses, the Kenans, completely imbued with the teachings of the Church, which says that the doctrine of Jesus accords with difficulty with our conceptions of life, tell us very seriously that the doctrine of Jesus is the doctrine of a visionary, the consolation of feeble minds; that it was all very well preached in the fishermen's huts by Galilee; but that for us it is only the sweet dream of one whom Kenan calls the *"charmant docteur."*

In their opinion, Jesus could not rise to the heights of wisdom and culture attained by our civilization. If he had been on an intellectual level with his modern critics, he never would have uttered his charming nonsense about the birds of the air, the turning of the other cheek, the taking no thought for the morrow. These historical critics judge the value of Christianity by what they see of it as it now exists. The Christianity of our age and civilization approves of society as it now is, with its prison cells, its factories, its houses of infamy, its parliaments; but as for the doctrine of Jesus, which is opposed to modern society, it is only empty words. The historical critics see this, and, unlike the so-called believers, having no motives for concealment, submit the doctrine to a careful analysis; they refute it systematically, and prove that Christianity is made up of nothing but chimerical ideas.

It would seem that before deciding upon the doctrine of Jesus, it would be necessary to understand of what it consisted; and to decide whether his doctrine is reasonable or not, it would be well first to realize that he said exactly what he did say. And this is precisely what we do not do, what the Church commentators do not do, what the free thinkers do not do and we know very well why. We know perfectly well that the doctrine of Jesus is directed at and denounces all human errors, all *tohu*, all the empty idols that we try to except from the category of errors, by dubbing them "Church," "State," "Culture," "Science," "Art," Civilization." But Jesus spoke precisely of all these, of these and all other *tohu*. Not only Jesus, but all the Hebrew prophets, John the Baptist, all the true sages of the world denounced the Church and State and culture and civilization of their times as sources of man's perdition.

Imagine an architect who says to a house-owner, "Your house is good for nothing; you must rebuild it," and then describes how the supports are to be cut and fastened. The proprietor turns a deaf ear to the words, "Your house is good for nothing," and only listens respectfully when the architect begins to discuss the arrangement of the rooms. Evidently, in this case, all the subsequent advice of the architect will seem to be impracticable; less respectful proprietors would regard it as nonsensical. But it is precisely in this way that we treat the doctrine of Jesus. I give this illustration for want of a better. I remember now that Jesus in teaching his doctrine made use of the same comparison. "Destroy this temple," he said, "and in three days I will raise it up." It was for this they put him on the cross, and for this they now crucify his doctrine.

The least that can be asked of those who pass judgment upon any doctrine is that they shall judge of it with the same understanding as that with which it was propounded. Jesus understood his doctrine, not as a vague and distant ideal impossible of attainment, not as a collection of fantastic and poetical reveries with which to charm the simple inhabitants on the shores of Galilee; to him his doctrine was a doctrine of action, of acts which should become the salvation of mankind. This he showed in his manner of applying his doctrine. The crucified one who cried out in agony of spirit and died for his doctrine was not a dreamer; he was a man of action. They are not dreamers who have died, and still die, for his doctrine. No; that doctrine is not a chimera!

All doctrine that reveals the truth is chimerical to the blind. We may say, as many people do say (I was of the number), that the doctrine of Jesus is chimerical because it is contrary to human nature. It is against nature, we say, to turn the other cheek when we have been struck, to give all that we possess, to toil, not for ourselves, but for others. It is natural, we say, for a man to defend his person, his family, his property; that is to say, it is the nature of man to struggle for existence. A learned person has prayed scientifically that the most sacred duty of man is to defend his rights, that is, to fight.

But the moment we detach ourselves from the idea that the existing organization established by man is the best, is sacred, the moment we do this, the objection that the doctrine of Jesus is contrary to human nature turns immediately upon him who makes it. No one will deny that not only to kill or torture a man, but to torture a dog, to kill a fowl or a calf, to inflict suffering is repugnant to human nature. (I have known of farmers who had ceased to eat meat solely because it had fallen to their lot to slaughter animals.) And yet our existence is so organized that every personal enjoyment is purchased at the price of human suffering contrary to human nature.

We have only to examine closely the complicated mechanism of our institutions that are based upon coercion to realize that coercion and violence are contrary to human nature. The judge who has condemned according to the code, is not willing to hang the criminal with his own hands; no clerk would tear a villager from his weeping family and cast him into prison; the general or the soldier, unless he be hardened by discipline and service, will not undertake to slay a hundred Turks or Germans or destroy a village, would not, if he could help it, kill a single man. Yet all these things are done, thanks to the administrative machinery which divides responsibility for misdeeds in such a way that no one feels them to be contrary to nature.

Some make the laws, others execute them; some train men by discipline to automatic obedience; and these last, in their turn, become the instruments of coercion, and slay their kind without knowing why or to what end. But let a man disentangle himself for a moment from this complicated network, and he will readily see that coercion is contrary to his nature. Let us abstain from affirming that organized violence, of which we make use to our own profit, is a divine, immutable law, and we shall see clearly which is most in harmony with human nature, the doctrine of violence or the doctrine of Jesus. What is the law of nature? Is it to know that my security and that of my family, all my amusements and pleasures, are purchased at the expense of misery, deprivation, and suffering to thousands of human beings by the terror of the gallows; by the misfortune of thousands stifling within prison walls; by the fear inspired by millions of soldiers and guardians of civilization, torn from their homes and besotted by discipline, to protect our pleasures with loaded revolvers against the possible interference of the famishing? Is it to purchase every fragment of bread that I put in my mouth and the mouths of my children by the numberless privations that are necessary to procure my abundance? Or is it to be certain that my piece of bread only belongs to me when I know that every one else has a share, and that no one starves while I eat?

It is only necessary to understand that, thanks to our social organization, each one of our pleasures, every minute of our cherished tranquillity, is obtained by the sufferings and privations of thousands of our fellows it is only necessary to understand this, to know what is conformable to human nature; not to our animal nature alone, but the animal and spiritual nature which constitutes man. When we once understand the doctrine of Jesus in all its bearings, with all its consequences, we shall be convinced that his doctrine is not contrary to human nature; but that its sole object is to supplant the chimerical law of the struggle against evil by violence itself the law contrary to human nature and productive of so many evils.

Do you say that the doctrine of Jesus, "Resist not evil" is vain? What, then, are we to think of the lives of those who are not filled with love and compassion for their kind, of those who make ready for their fellow men punishment at the stake, by the knout, the wheel, the rack, chains, compulsory labor, the gibbet, dungeons, prisons for women and children, the hecatombs of war, or bring about periodical revolutions; of those who carry these horrors into execution; of those who benefit by these calamities or prepare reprisals, are not such lives vain?

We need only understand the doctrine of Jesus, to be convinced that existence, not the reasonable existence which gives happiness to humanity, but the existence men have organized to their own hurt, that such an existence is a vanity, the most savage and horrible of vanities, a veritable delirium of folly, to which, once reclaimed, we do not again return.

God descended to earth, became incarnate to redeem Adam's sin, and (so we were taught to believe) said many mysterious and mystical things which are difficult to understand, which it is not possible to understand except by the aid of faith and grace and suddenly the words of God are found to be simple, clear, and reasonable! God said, Do no evil, and evil will cease to exist. Was the revelation from God really so simple nothing but that? It would seem that every one might understand it, it is so simple!

The prophet Elijah, a fugitive from men, took refuge in a cave, and was told that God would appear to him. There came a great wind that devastated the forest; Elijah thought that the Lord had come, but the Lord was not in the wind. After the wind came the thunder and the lightning, but God was not there. Then came the earthquake: the earth belched forth (ire, the rocks were shattered, the mountain was rent to its foundations; Elijah looked for the Lord, but the Lord was not in the earthquake. Then, in the calm that followed, a gentle breeze came to the prophet, bearing the freshness of the fields; and Elijah knew that God was there. It is a magnificent illustration of the words, "Resist not evil."

They are very simple, these words; but they are, nevertheless, the expression of a law divine and human. If there has been in history a progressive movement for the suppression of evil, it is due to the men who understood the doctrine of Jesus who endured evil, and resisted not evil by violence. The advance of humanity towards righteousness is due, not to the tyrants, but to the martyrs. As fire cannot extinguish fire, so evil cannot suppress evil. Good alone, confronting evil and resisting its contagion, can overcome evil. And in the inner world of the human soul, the law is as absolute as was even the law of Galileo, more absolute, more clear, more immutable. Men may turn aside from it, they may hide its truth from others; but the progress of humanity towards righteousness can only be attained in this way. Every step must be guided by the command, "Resist not evil." A disciple of Jesus may say no with greater assurance than did Galileo, in spite of misfortunes and threats: "And yet it is not violence, but good, that overcomes evil." If the progress is slow, it is because the doctrine of Jesus (which, through its clearness, simplicity, and wisdom, appeals so inevitably to human nature), because the doctrine of Jesus has been cunningly concealed from the majority of mankind under an entirely different doctrine falsely called by his name.

Chapter 5

THE TRUE MEANING of the doctrine of Jesus was revealed to me; everything confirmed its truth. But for a long time I could not accustom myself to the strange fact, that after the eighteen centuries during which the law of Jesus had been professed by millions of human beings, after the eighteen centuries during which thousands of men had consecrated their lives to the study of this law, I had discovered it for myself anew. But strange as it seemed, so it was. Christ's teaching, "Resist not evil," was to me wholly new, something of which I had never had any conception before. I asked myself how this could be; I must certainly have had a false idea of the doctrine of Jesus to cause such a misunderstanding. And a false idea of it I unquestionably had. When I began to read the Gospel, I was not in the condition of one who, having heard nothing of the doctrine of Jesus, becomes acquainted with it for the first time; on the contrary, I had a preconceived theory as to the manner in which I ought to understand it. Jesus did not appeal to me as a prophet revealing the divine law, but as one who continued and amplified the absolute divine law which I already knew; for I had very definite and complex notions about God, the creator of the world and of man, and about the commandments of God given to men through the instrumentality of Moses.

When I came to the words, "Ye have heard that it hath been said, An eye for an eye, and a tooth for a tooth: But I say unto you, That ye resist not evil," the words, "An eye for an eye, and a tooth for a tooth," expressed the law given by God to Moses; the words, "But I say unto you, That ye resist not evil," expressed the new law, which was a negation of the first. If I had seen Jesus words, simply, in their true sense, and not as a part of the theological theory that I had imbibed at my mother's breast, I should have understood immediately that Jesus abrogated the old law, and substituted for it a new law. But I had been taught that Jesus did not abrogate the Law of Moses, that, on the contrary, he confirmed it to the slightest iota, and that he made it more complete. Verses 17–20 of the fifth chapter of Matthew always impressed me, when I read the Gospel, by their obscurity, and they plunged me into doubt. I knew the Old Testament, particularly the last books of Moses, very thoroughly, and recalling certain passages in which minute doctrines, often absurd and even cruel in their purport, are preceded by the words, "And the Lord said unto Moses," it seemed to me very singular that Jesus should confirm all these injunctions; I could not understand why he did so. But I allowed the question to pass without solution, and accepted with confidence the explanations inculcated in my infancy, that the two laws were equally inspired by the Holy Spirit, that they were in perfect accord, and that Jesus confirmed the law of Moses while completing and amplifying it. I did not concern myself with accounting for the process of this amplification, with the solution of the contradictions apparent throughout the whole Gospel, in verses 17–20 of the fifth chapter, in the words, "But I say unto you."

Now that I understood the clear and simple meaning of the doctrine of Jesus, I saw clearly that the two laws are directly opposed to one another; that they can never be harmonized; that, instead of supplementing one by the other, we must inevitably choose between the two; and that the received explanation of the verses, Matthew v. 17–20, which had impressed me by their obscurity, must be incorrect.

When I now came to read once more the verses that had before impressed me as obscure, I was astonished at the clear and simple meaning which was suddenly revealed to me. This meaning was revealed, not by any combination and transposition, but solely by rejecting the factitious explanations with which the words had been encumbered. According to Matthew, Jesus said (v. 17–18):

"Think not that I am come to destroy the law, or the prophets (the doctrine of the prophets): I do not come to destroy, but to fulfil. For verily I say unto you, till heaven and earth pass, one jot or one tittle shall in no wise pass from the law, till all be fulfiled."

And in verse 20 he added: "For I say unto you, that except your righteousness shall exceed the righteousness of the scribes and Pharisees, ye shall in no case enter into the kingdom of heaven."

I am not come (Jesus said) to destroy the eternal law of whose fulfilment your books of prophecy fore tell. I am come to teach you the fulfilment of the eternal law; not of the law that your scribes and Pharisees call the divine law, but of that eternal law which is more immutable than the earth and the heavens.

I have expressed the idea in other words in order to detach the thoughts of my readers from the traditional false interpretation. If this false interpretation had never existed, the idea expressed in the verses could not be rendered in a better or more definite manner.

The view that Jesus did not abrogate the old law arises from the arbitrary conclusion that "law" in this passage signifies the written law instead of the law eternal, the reference to the iota jot and tittle perhaps furnishing the grounds for such an opinion. But if Jesus had been speaking of the written law, he would have used the "expression the law and the prophets," which he always employed in speaking of the written law; here, however, he uses a different expression, "the law or the prophets." If Jesus had meant the written law, he would have used the expression, "the law and the prophets," in the verses that follow and that continue the thought; but he says, briefly, "the law." Moreover, according to Luke, Jesus made use of the same phraseology, and the context renders the meaning inevitable. According to Luke, Jesus said to the Pharisees, who assumed the justice of their written law:

He says: You justify yourselves before men; but God knoweth your hearts: for that which is highly esteemed among men is abomination in the sight of God. The law and the prophets were until John: since that time the kingdom of God is preached, and every man presseth into it. And it is easier for heaven and earth to pass, than one tittle of the law to fail." (Luke xvi. 15–17.)

In the words, "The law and the prophets were until John," Jesus abrogated the written law; in the words, "And it is easier for heaven and earth to pass, than one tittle of the law to fail," Jesus confirmed the law eternal. In the first passage cited he said, "the law and the prophets," that is, the written law; in the second he said "the law" simply, therefore the law eternal. It is clear, then, that the eternal law is opposed to the written law, exactly as in the context of Matthew where the eternal law is defined by the phrase, "the law or the prophets."

The history of the variants of the text of these verses is quite worthy of notice. The majority of texts have simply "the law," without the addition, "and the prophets," thus avoiding a false interpretation in the sense of the written law. In other texts, notably that of Tischendorf, and in the canonical versions, we find the word "prophets" used, not with the conjunction "and," but with the con junction "or," "the law or the prophets," which also excludes any question of the written law, and indicates, as the proper signification, the law eternal. In several other versions, not countenanced by the Church, we find the word "prophets "used with the conjunction "and," not with "or"; and in these versions every repetition of the words "the law "is followed by the phrase, "and the prophets," which would indicate that Jesus spoke only of the written law.

The history of the commentaries on the passage in question coincides with that of the variants. The only clear meaning is that authorized by Luke, that Jesus spoke of the eternal law. But among the copyists of the Gospel were some who desired that the written Law of Moses should continue to be regarded as obligatory. They therefore added to the words "the law "the phrase "and the prophets," and thereby changed the interpretation of the text.

Other Christians, not recognizing to the same degree the authority of the books of Moses, suppressed the added phrase, and replaced the particle *kai*, "and," with "or"; and with this substitution the passage was admitted to the canon. Nevertheless, in spite of the unequivocal clearness of the text as thus written, the commentators perpetuated the interpretation supported by the phrase which had been rejected in the canon. The passage evoked innumerable comments, which stray from the true signification in proportion to the lack, en the part of the commentators, of fidelity to the simple and obvious meaning of Jesus doctrine. Most of them recognize the reading rejected by the canonical text.

To be absolutely convinced that Jesus spoke only of the eternal law, we need only examine the true meaning of the word which has given rise to so many false interpretations. The word

"law" (in Greek νομος, in Hebrew, *torah*) has in all languages two
principal meanings: one, law in the abstract sense, independent
of formulae; the other, the written statutes which men generally
recognize as law. In the Greek of Paul's Epistles the distinction
is indicated by the use of the article. Without the article Paul
uses νομος the most frequently in the sense of the divine eternal
law. By the ancient Hebrews, as in books of Isaiah and the other
prophets, the *torah*, is always used in the sense of an eternal revelation, a divine intuition. It was not till the time of Esdras, and
later in the Talmud, that "*Torah*" was used in the same sense in
which we use the word "Bible" with this difference, that while we
have words to distinguish between the Bible and the divine law,
the Jews employed the same word to express both meanings.

And so Jesus sometimes speaks of law as the divine law (of
Isaiah and the other prophets), in which case he confirms it; and
sometimes in the sense of the written law of the Pentateuch, in
which case he rejects it. To distinguish the difference he always,
in speaking of the written law, adds, "and the prophets," or pre-
fixes the word "your" or "your law." When he says: "Therefore
all things whatsoever ye would that men should do to you, do
ye even so to them: For this is the law and the prophets," (Matt.
vii. 12), he speaks of the written law. The entire written law, he
says, may be reduced to this expression of the eternal law, and by
these words he abrogated the written law. When he says, "The
law and the prophets were until John," (Luke xvi. 16), he speaks of
the written law, and abrogates it. When he says, "Did not Moses
give you the law? – And yet none of you keepeth the law," (John
vii. 19), "It is also written in your law" (John viii. 17), ("that the
word might be fulfiled that is written in their law" (John xv. 25),
he speaks of the written law, the law whose authority he denied,
the law that condemned him to death: "The Jews answered him
We have a law, and by our law he ought to die," (John xix. 7). It
is plain that this Jewish law, which authorized condemnation to
death, was not the law of Jesus. But when Jesus says, "I come not
to destroy the law, but to teach you the fulfilment of the law: For
nothing of this law shall be changed, but all shall be fulfiled."
Of this he speaks, not of the written law, but of the divine and
eternal law.

Admit that all this is merely formal proof; admit that I have carefully combined contexts and variants, and excluded everything contrary to my theory; admit that the commentators of the Church are clear and convincing, that, in fact, Jesus did not abrogate the law of Moses, but upheld it; admit this – then the question is, what were the teachings of Jesus?

According to the Church, he taught that he was the second person of the Trinity, the Son of God, and that he came into the world to atone by his death for Adam's sin. Those, however, who have read the Gospels know that Jesus taught nothing of the sort, or at least spoke but very vaguely on these topics. The passages in which Jesus affirms that he is the second person of the Trinity, and that he was to atone for the sins of humanity, form a very inconsiderable and obscure portion of the Gospels. In what, then, does the rest of Jesus doctrine consist? It is impossible to deny, for all Christians have recognized the fact, that the doctrine of Jesus aims summarily to regulate the lives of men, to teach them how they ought to live with regard to one another. But to realize that Jesus taught men a new way of life, we must have some idea of the condition of the people to whom his teachings were addressed.

When we examine into the social development of the Russians, the English, the Chinese, the Indians, or even the races of insular savages, we find that each people invariably has certain practical rules or laws which govern its existence; consequently, if anyone would inculcate a new law, he must at the same time abolish the old; in any race or nation this would be inevitable. Laws that we are accustomed to regard as almost sacred would assuredly be abrogated; with us, perhaps, it might happen that a reformer who taught a new law would abolish only our civil laws, the official code, our administrative customs, without touching what we consider as our divine laws, although it is difficult to believe that such could be the case. But with the Jewish people, who had but one law, and that recognized as divine, a law which enveloped life to its minutest details, what could a reformer accomplish if he declared in advance that the existing law was inviolable?

Admit that this argument is not conclusive, and try to interpret the words of Jesus as an affirmation of the entire Mosaic law; in that case, who were the Pharisees, the scribes, the doctors of the law?, denounced by Jesus during the whole of his ministry? Who were they that rejected the doctrine of Jesus and, their High Priests at their head, crucified him? If Jesus approved the Law of Moses, where were the faithful followers of that law, who practised it sincerely, and must thereby have obtained Jesus approval? Is it possible that there was not one such? The Pharisees, we are told, constituted a sect; where, then, were the righteous?

In the Gospel of John the enemies of Jesus are spoken of directly as "the Jews." They are opposed to the doctrine of Jesus; they are hostile because they are Jews. But it is not only the Pharisees and the Sadducees who figure in the Gospels as the enemies of Jesus: we also find mention of the doctors of the law, the guardians of the law of Moses, the scribes, the interpreters of the law, the ancients, those who are always considered as representatives of the people's wisdom. Jesus said, "I am not come to call the righteous, but sinners to repentance," to change their way of life. But where were the righteous? Was Nicodemus the only one? He is represented as a good, but misguided man.

We are so habituated to the singular opinion that Jesus was crucified by the Pharisees and a number of Jewish shopkeepers, that we never think to ask, Where were the true Jews, the good Jews, the Jews that practised the law? When we have once propounded this query, everything becomes perfectly clear. Jesus, whether he was God or man, brought his doctrine to a people possessing rules, called the divine law, governing their whole existence. How could Jesus avoid denouncing that law?

Every prophet, every founder of a religion, inevitably meets, in revealing the divine law to men, with institutions which are regarded as upheld by the laws of God. He cannot, therefore, avoid a double use of the word "law," which expresses what his hearers wrongfully consider the law of God "your law;" and the law he has come to proclaim, the true law, the divine and eternal law. A reformer not only cannot avoid the use of the word in this manner; often he does not wish to avoid it, but purposely confounds the two ideas, thus indicating that, in the law confessed by those whom he would convert, there are still some eternal truths.

Every reformer takes these truths, so well known to his hearers, as the basis of his teaching. This is precisely what Jesus did in addressing the Jews, by whom the two laws were vaguely grouped together as "*Torah.*" Jesus recognized that the Mosaic law, and still more the prophetical books, especially the writings of Isaiah, whose words he constantly quotes, Jesus recognized that these contained divine and eternal truths in harmony with the eternal law, and these he takes as the basis of his own doctrine. This method was many times referred to by Jesus; thus he said, "What is written in the law? How readest thou?" (Luke x. 26). That is, one may find eternal truth in the law, if one reads it aright. And more than once he affirms that the commandments of the Mosaic law, to love the Lord and one's neighbor, are also commandments of the eternal law. At the conclusion of the parables by which Jesus explained the meaning of his doctrine to his disciples, he pronounced words that have a bearing upon all that precedes:

"*Therefore every scribe which is instructed unto the kingdom of heaven (the truth) is like unto a man that is a householder, which bringeth forth out of his treasure (without distinction) things new and old." (Matt. xiii. 52.)*

The Church understands these words, as they were understood by Irenaeus; but at the same time, in defiance of the true signification, it arbitrarily attributes to them the meaning that everything old is sacred. The manifest meaning is this: He who seeks for the good, takes not only the new, but also the old; and because a thing is old, he does not therefore reject it. By these words Jesus meant that he did not deny what was eternal in the old law but when they spoke to him of the whole law, or of the formalities exacted by the old law, his reply was that new wine should not be put into old bottles. Jesus could not affirm the whole law; neither could he deny the entire teachings of the law and the prophets, the law which says, "*love thy neighbor as thyself,*" the prophets whose words often served to express his own thoughts. And yet, in place of this clear and simple explanation of Jesus words, we are offered a vague interpretation which introduces needless contradictions, which reduces the doctrine of Jesus to nothingness, and which re-establishes the doctrine of Moses in all its savage cruelty.

Commentators of the Church, particularly those who have written since the fifth century, tell us that Jesus did not abolish the written law; that, on the contrary, he affirmed it. But in what way? How is it possible that the law of Jesus should harmonize with the Law of Moses? To these inquiries we get no response.

The commentators all make use of a verbal juggle to the effect that Jesus fulfilled the law of Moses, and that the sayings of the prophets were fulfilled in his person; that Jesus fulfilled the law as our mediator by our faith in him. And the essential question for every believer how to harmonize two conflicting laws, each designed to regulate the lives of men, is left without the slightest attempt at explanation. Thus the contradiction between the verse where it is said that Jesus did not come to destroy the law, but to fulfil the law, and Jesus saying, "Ye have heard that it hath been said, An eye for an eye . . . But I say unto you," the contradiction between the doctrine of Jesus and the very spirit of the Mosaic doctrine, is left without any mitigation.

Let those who are interested in the question look through the Church commentaries touching this passage from the time of Chrysostom to our day. After a perusal of the voluminous explanations offered, they will be convinced not only of the complete absence of any solution for the contradiction, but of the presence of a new, factitious contradiction arising in its place. Let us see what Chrysostom says in reply to those who reject the Law of Moses:

"He made this law, not that we might strike out one another's eyes, but that fear of suffering by others might restrain us from doing any such thing to them. As therefore He threatened the Ninevites with overthrow, not that He might destroy them (for had that been His will, He ought to have been silent), but that He might by fear make them better, and so quiet His wrath: so also hath he appointed a punishment for those who wantonly assail the eyes of others, that if good principle dispose them not to refrain from such cruelty, fear may restrain them from injuring their neighbors sight.

"And if this be cruelty, it is cruelty also for the murderer to be restrained, and the adulterer checked. But these are the sayings of senseless men, and of those that are mad to the extreme of madness. For I, so far from saying that this comes of cruelly, should say that the contrary to this would be unlawful, according to men's reckoning. And whereas thou sayest, Because He commanded to pluck out an eye for an eye, therefore He is cruel; I say that if He had not given this commandment, then He would have seemed, in the judgment of most men, to be that which thou sayest He is."

Chrysostom clearly recognized the law, An eye for an eye, as divine, and the contrary of that law, that is, the doctrine of Jesus, Resist not evil, as an iniquity. "For let us suppose," says Chrysostom further:

"For let us suppose that this law had been altogether done away, and that no one feared the punishment ensuing thereupon, but that license had been given to all the wicked to follow their own dispositions in all security, to adulterers, and to murderers, to perjured persons, and to parricides; would not all things have been turned upside down, and would not cities, market places and houses, sea and land, and the whole world have been filled with unnumbered pollution's and murders? Everyone sees it. For if, when there are laws, and fear, and threatening, our evil dispositions are hardly checked; were even this security taken away, what is there to prevent men's choosing vice and what degree of mischief would not then come revelling upon the whole of human life?

"That rather, since cruelty lies not only in allowing the bad to do what they will, but in another thing too quite as much, to overlook, and leave uncared for, him who hath done no wrong, but who is without cause or reason suffering ill. For tell me; were anyone to gather together wicked men from all quarters, and arm them with swords, and bid them go about the whole city, and massacre all that came in their way, could there be anything more like a wild beast than he? And what if some others should bind, and confine with the utmost strictness, those whom that man had armed, and should snatch from those lawless hands them who were on the point of being butchered; could any thing be greater humanity than this?"

Chrysostom does not say what would be the estimate of these others in the opinion of the wicked. And what if these others were themselves wicked and cast the innocent into prison?

Chrysostom continues: "Now then, I bid thee transfer these examples to the Law likewise; for He that commands to pluck out *an eye for an eye* hath laid the fear as a kind of strong chain upon the souls of the bad, and so resembles him who detains those assassins in prison; whereas he who appoints no punishment for them, doth all but arm them by such security, and acts the part of that other, who was putting the swords in their hands, and letting them loose over the whole city." (*Homilies on the Gospel of St. Matthew*, xvi.)

If Chrysostom had understood the law of Jesus, he would have said, who is it that strikes out another's eyes? Who is it that casts men into prison? If God, who made the law, does this, then there is no contradiction; but it is men who carry out the decrees, and the Son of God has said to men that they must abstain from violence. God commanded to strike out, and the Son of God commanded not to strike out. We must accept one commandment or the other; and Chrysostom, like all the rest of the Church, accepted the commandment of Moses and denied that of the Christ, whose doctrine he nevertheless claims to believe.

Jesus abolished the Mosaic law, and gave his own law in its place. To one who really believes in Jesus there is not the slightest contradiction; such a person will pay no attention to the Law of Moses, but will practise the law of Jesus, which he believes. To one who believes in the Law of Moses there is no contradiction. The Jews looked upon the words of Jesus as foolishness, and believed in the Law of Moses. The contradiction is only for those who would follow the Law of Moses under the cover of the law of Jesus for those whom Jesus denounced as hypocrites, as a generation of vipers.

Instead of recognizing as divine truth the one or the other of the two laws, the Law of Moses or that of Jesus, we recognize the divine quality of both. But when the question comes with regard to the acts of everyday life, we reject the law of Jesus and follow that of Moses. And this false interpretation, when we realize its importance, reveals the source of that terrible drama which records the struggle between evil and good, between darkness and light.

To the Jewish people, trained to the innumerable formal regulations instituted by the Levites, in the rubric of divine laws, each preceded by the words, "And the Lord said unto Moses" . . . to the Jewish people Jesus appeared. He found everything, to the minutest detail, prescribed by rule; not only the relation of man with God, but his sacrifices, his feasts, his fasts, his social, civil, and family duties, the details of personal habits, circumcision, the purification of the body, of domestic utensils, of clothing all these regulated by laws recognized as commandments of God, and therefore as divine.

Excluding the question of Jesus divine mission, what could any prophet or reformer do who wished to establish his own doctrines among a people so enveloped in formalism what but abolish the law by which all these details were regulated? Jesus selected from what men considered as the law of God the portions which were really divine; he took what served his purpose, rejected the rest, and upon this foundation established the eternal law. It was not necessary to abolish all, but inevitable to abrogate much that was looked upon as obligatory. This Jesus did, and was accused of destroying the divine law; for this lie was condemned and put to death. But his doctrine was cherished by his disciples, traversed the centuries, and is transmitted to other peoples. Under these conditions it is again hidden beneath heterogeneous dogmas, obscure comments, and factitious explanations. Pitiable human sophisms replace the divine revelation. For the formula, "And the Lord said unto Moses," we substitute "Thus saith the Holy Spirit." And again formalism hides the truth. Most astounding of all, the doctrine of Jesus is amalgamated with the written law, whose authority he was forced to deny. This *Torah*, this written law, is declared to have been inspired by the Holy Spirit, the spirit of truth; and thus Jesus is taken in the snare of his own revelation his doctrine is reduced to nothingness.

This is why, after eighteen hundred years, it so singularly happened that I discovered the meaning of the doctrine of Jesus as some new thing. But no; I did not discover it; I did simply what all must do who seek after God and His law; I sought for the eternal law amid the incongruous elements that men call by that name.

Chapter 6

WHEN I UNDERSTOOD the law of Jesus as the law of Jesus, and not as the law of Jesus and of Moses, when I understood the commandment of this law which absolutely abrogated the law of Moses, then the Gospels, before to me so obscure, diffuse, and contradictory, blended into a harmonious whole, the substance of whose doctrine, until then incomprehensible, I found to be formulated in terms simple, clear, and accessible to every searcher after truth.

Throughout the Gospels we are called upon to consider the commandments of Jesus and the necessity of practising them. All the theologians discuss the commandments of Jesus; but what are these commandments? I did not know before. I thought that the commandment of Jesus was to love God, and one's neighbor as one's self. I did not see that this could not be a new commandment of Jesus, since it was given by them of old in Deuteronomy and Leviticus. The words:

"Whosoever therefore shall break one of these least commandments, and shall teach men so, he shall be called the least in the kingdom of heaven: but whosoeve shall do and teach them, the same shall be called great in the kingdom of heaven," (Matt. v. 19.) these words I believed to relate to the Mosaic law. But it never had occurred to me that Jesus had propounded, clearly and precisely, new laws. I did not see that in the passage where Jesus declares, "Ye have heard that it was said . . . But I say unto you," he formulated a series of very definite commandments, five entirely new, counting as one the two references to the ancient law against adultery. I had heard of the beatitudes of Jesus and of their number; their explanation and enumeration had formed a part of my religious instruction; but the commandments of Jesus I had never heard them spoken of. To my great astonishment, I now discovered them for myself. In the fifth chapter of Matthew I found these verses:

"Ye have heard that it was said by them of old time, Thou shalt not kill; and whosoever shall kill shall be in danger of the judgment: But I say unto you, That whosoever is angry with his brother

without a cause shall be in danger of the judgment: and who so ever shall say to his brother, Raca, shall be in danger of the council: but whosoever shall say, Thou fool, shall be in danger of the Gehenna of fire. Therefore if thou bring thy gift to the altar, and there remember that thy brother hath aught against thee; Leave there thy gift before the altar, and go thy way; first be reconciled to thy brother, and then come and offer thy gift. Agree with thine adversary quickly, while thou art in the way with him; lest at any time the adversary deliver thee to the judge, and the judge deliver thee to the officer, and thou be cast into prison. Verily I say unto thee, Thou shalt by no means come out thence, till thou hast paid the uttermost farthing." (Matt. v. 21–26.)

When I understood the commandment, "Resist not evil," it seemed to me that these verses must have a meaning as clear and intelligible as has the commandment just cited. The meaning I had formerly given to the passage was, that every one ought to avoid angry feelings against others, ought never to utter abusive language, and ought to live in peace with all men, without exception. But there was in the text a phrase which excluded this meaning, "Whosoever shall be angry with his brother without a cause" the words could not then be an exhortation to absolute peace. I was greatly perplexed, and I turned to the commentators, the theologians, for the removal of my doubts. To my surprise I found that the commentators were chiefly occupied with the endeavor to define under what conditions anger was permissible. All the commentators of the Church dwelt upon the qualifying phrase "without a cause," and explained the meaning to be that one must not be offended without a reason, that one must not be abusive, but that anger is not always unjust; and, to confirm their view, they quoted instances of anger on the part of saints and apostles. I saw plainly that the commentators who authorized anger "for the glory of God" as not reprehensible, although entirely contrary to the spirit of the Gospel, based their argument on the phrase "without a cause," in the twenty-second verse. These words change entirely the meaning of the passage.

"Be not angry without cause." Jesus exhorts us to pardon everyone, to pardon without restriction or limit. He pardoned all who did him wrong, and chided Peter for being angry with

Malchus when the former sought to defend his Master at the time of the betrayal, when, if at any time, it would seem that anger might have been justifiable. And yet did this same Jesus formally teach men not to be angry without a cause," and thereby sanction anger for a cause? Did Jesus enjoin peace upon all men, and then, in the phrase "without a cause," interpolate the reservation that this rule did not apply to all cases; that there were circumstances under which one might be angry with a brother, and so give the commentators the right to say that anger is sometimes expedient?

But who is to decide when anger is expedient and when it is not expedient? I never yet encountered an angry person who did not believe his wrath to be justifiable. Every one who is angry thinks anger legitimate and serviceable. Evidently the qualifying phrase "without a cause" destroys the entire force of the verse. And yet there were the words in the sacred text, and I could not efface them. The effect was the same as if the word "good" had been added to the phrase. "Love thy neighbor"– love thy good neighbor, the neighbor that agrees with thee!

The entire signification of the passage was changed by this phrase, "without a cause." Verses 23 and 24, which exhort us to be reconciled with all men before appealing for divine aid, also lost their direct and imperative meaning and acquired a conditional import through the influence of the foregoing qualification. It had seemed to me, however, that Jesus forbade all anger, all evil sentiment, and, that it might not continue in our hearts, exhorted us before entering into communion with God to ask ourselves if there were any person who might be angry with us. If such were the case, whether this anger were with cause or without cause, he commanded us to be reconciled. In this manner I had interpreted the passage; but it now seemed, according to the commentators, that the injunction must be taken as a conditional affirmation. The commentators all explained that we ought to try to be at peace with everybody; but, they added, if this is impossible, if, actuated by evil instincts, anyone is at enmity with you, try to be reconciled with him in spirit, in idea, and then the enmity of others will be no obstacle to divine communion.

Nor was this all. The words, "Whosoever shall say to his brother, *Raca*, shall be in danger of the council," always seemed to me strange and absurd. If we are forbidden to be abusive, why this example with its ordinary and harmless epithet; why this terrible threat against those that utter abuse so feeble as that implied in the word Raca, which means you good-for-nothing? All this was obscure to me.

I was convinced that I had before me a problem similar to that which had confronted me in the words, "Judge not." I felt that here again the simple, grand, precise, and practical meaning of Jesus had been hidden, and that the commentators were groping in gloom. It seemed to me that Jesus, in saying, "be reconciled to thy brother," could not have meant, "be reconciled in idea," an explanation not at all clear, supposing it were true. I understood what Jesus meant when, using the words of the prophet, he said, "will have mercy, and not sacrifice;" that is, "I will that men shall love one another. If you would have your acts acceptable to God, then, before offering prayer, interrogate your conscience; and if you find that anyone is angry with you, go and make your peace with him, and then pray as you desire." After this clear interpretation, what was I to understand by the comment, "be reconciled in idea"?

I saw that what seemed to me the only clear and direct meaning of the verse was destroyed by the phrase, "without a cause." If I could eliminate that, there would be no difficulty in the way of a lucid interpretation. But all the commentators were united against any such course; and the canonical text authorized the rendering to which I objected. I could not drop these words arbitrarily, and yet, if they were excluded, everything would become clear. I therefore sought for some interpretation which would not conflict with the sense of the entire passage.

I consulted the dictionary. In ordinary Greek, the word εἰχη means "heedlessly, inconsiderately." I tried to find some term that would not destroy the sense; but the words, "without a cause," plainly had the meaning attributed to them. In New Testament Greek the signification of εἰχη is exactly the same. I consulted the concordances. The word occurs but once in the Gospels, namely, in this passage. In the first epistle to the Corinthians, xv.

2, it occurs in exactly the same sense. It is impossible to interpret it otherwise, and if we accept it, we must conclude that Jesus uttered in vague words a commandment easily so construed as to be of no effect. To admit this seemed to me equivalent to rejecting the entire Gospel. There remained one more resource was the word to be found in all the manuscripts? I consulted Griesbach, who records all recognized variants, and discovered to my joy that the passage in question was not invariable, and that the variation depended upon the word ειχη. In most of the Gospel texts and the citations of the Fathers, this word does not occur. I consulted Tischendorf for the most ancient reading: the word ειχη did not appear.

This word, so destructive to the meaning of the doctrine of Jesus, is then an interpolation which had not crept into the best copies of the Gospel as late as the fifth century. Some copyist added the word; others approved it and undertook its explanation. Jesus did not utter, could not have uttered, this terrible word; and the primary meaning of the passage, its simple, direct, impressive meaning, is the true interpretation.

Now that I understood Jesus to forbid anger, whatever the cause, and without distinction of persons, the warning against the use of the words "raca" and "fool" had a purport quite distinct from any prohibition with regard to the utterance of abusive epithets. The strange Hebrew word, *Raca*, which is not translated in the Greek text, serves to reveal the meaning. *Raca* means, literally, "vain, empty, that which does not exist." It was much used by the Hebrews to express exclusion. It is employed in the plural form in Judges ix. 4, in the sense, "empty and vain." This word Jesus forbids us to apply to anyone, as he forbids us to use the word "fool," which, like "*Raca*," relieves us of all the obligations of humanity. We get angry, we do evil to men, and then to excuse ourselves we say that the object of our anger is an empty person, the refuse of a man, a fool. It is precisely such words as these that Jesus forbids us to apply to men. He exhorts us not to be angry with anyone, and not to excuse our anger with the plea that we have to do with a vain person, a person bereft of reason.

And so in place of insignificant, vague, and uncertain phrases subject to arbitrary interpretation, I found in Matthew v. 21–26 the first commandment of Jesus: Live in peace with all men. Do not regard anger as justifiable under any circumstances. Never look upon a human being as worthless or as a fool. Not only refrain from anger yourself, but do not regard the anger of others toward you as vain. If anyone is angry with you, even without reason, be reconciled to him, that all hostile feelings may be effaced. Agree quickly with those that have a grievance against you, lest animosity prevail to your loss.

The first commandment of Jesus being thus freed from obscurity, I was able to understand the second, which also begins with a reference to the ancient law:

"Ye have heard that it was said by them of old time, Thou shalt not commit adultery: But I say unto you, that whosoever looketh on a woman to lust after her hath committed adultery with her already in his heart. And if thy right eye offend thee pluck it out, and cast it from thee: for it is profitable for thee that one of thy members should perish, and not that thy whole body should be cast into hell. And if thy right hand offend thee, cut it off, and cast it from thee: for it is profitable for thee that one of thy members should perish, and not that thy whole body should be cast into hell." (Deut. xxiv. 1.) It hath been said, whosoever shall put away his wife, saving for the cause of fornication, causeth her to commit adultery: and whosoever shall marry her that is divorced committeth adultery. (Matt. v. 27–32.)

By these words I understood that a man ought not, even in imagination, to admit that he could approach any woman save her to whom he had once been united, and her he might never abandon to take another, although permitted to do so by the Mosaic law.

In the first commandment, Jesus counselled us to extinguish the germ of anger, and illustrated his meaning by the fate of the man who is delivered to the judges; in the second commandment Jesus declares that debauchery arises from the disposition of men and women to regard one another as instruments of voluptuousness, and, this being so we ought to guard against every idea that excites to sensual desire, and, once united to a woman, never to abandon her on any pretext, for women thus abandoned are sought by other men, and so debauchery is introduced into the world.

The wisdom of this commandment impressed me profoundly. It would suppress all the evils in the world that result from the sexual relations. Convinced that license in the sexual relations leads to contention, men, in obedience to this injunction, would avoid every cause for voluptuousness, and, knowing that the law of humanity is to live in couples, would so unite themselves, and never destroy the bond of union. All the evils arising from dissensions caused by sexual attraction would be suppressed, since there would be neither men nor women deprived of the sexual relation.

But I was much more impressed, as I read the Sermon on the Mount, with the words, "Saving for the cause of fornication," which permitted a man to repudiate his wife in case of infidelity. The very form in which the idea was expressed seemed to me unworthy of the dignity of the occasion, for here, side by side with the profound truths of the Sermon on the Mount, occurred, like a note in a criminal code, this strange exception to the general rule; but I shall not dwell upon the question of form; I shall speak only of the exception itself, so entirely in contradiction with the fundamental idea.

I consulted the commentators; all, Chrysostom and the others, even authorities on exegesis like Reuss, all recognized the meaning of the words to be that Jesus permitted divorce in case of infidelity on the part of the woman, and that, in the exhortation against divorce in the nineteenth chapter of Matthew, the same words had the same signification. I read the thirty-second verse of the fifth chapter again and again, and reason refused to accept the interpretation. To verify my doubts I consulted the other portions of the New Testament texts, and I found in Matthew (xix.), Mark (x.), Luke (xvi.), and in the first epistle of Paul to the Corinthians, affirmation of the doctrine of the indissolubility of marriage. In Luke (xvi. 18) it is said:

"Whosoever putteth away his wife, and marrieth another, committeth adultery: and whosoever marrieth her that is put away from her husband committeth adultery."

In Mark (x. 5–12) the doctrine is also proclaimed without any exception whatever:

"For the hardness of your heart he [Moses] wrote you this precept. But from the beginning of the creation God made them male and female. For this cause shall a man leave his father and mother, and cleave to his wife; and they twain shall be one flesh: so then they are no more twain, but one flesh. What therefore God hath joined together, let not man put asunder. And in the house his disciples asked him again of the same matter. And he said unto them, whosoever shall put away his wife, and marry another, committeth adultery against her. And if a woman shall put away her husband and be married to another, she committeth adultery."

The same idea is expressed in Matt. xix. 4–9. Paul, in the first epistle to the Corinthians (vii.–11), develops systematically the idea that the only way of preventing debauchery is that every man have his own wife, and every woman have her own husband, and that they mutually satisfy the sexual instinct; then he says, without equivocation, "Let not the wife depart from her husband: But and if she depart, let her remain unmarried, or be reconciled to her husband: and let not the husband put away his wife."

According to Mark, and Luke, and Paul, divorce is forbidden. It is forbidden by the assertion repeated in two of the Gospels that husband and wife are one flesh whom God hath joined together. It is forbidden by the doctrine of Jesus, who exhorts us to pardon everyone, without excepting the adulterous woman. It is forbidden by the general sense of the whole passage, which explains that divorce is provocative of debauchery, and for this reason that divorce with an adulterous woman is prohibited.

Upon what, then, is based the opinion that divorce is permissible in case of infidelity on the part of the woman? Upon the words which had so impressed me in Matt. v. 32; the words every one takes to mean that Jesus permits divorce in case of adultery by the woman; the words, repeated in Matt. xix. 9, in a number of copies of the Gospel text, and by many Fathers of the Church, the words, "unless for the cause of adultery." I studied these words carefully anew. For a long time I could not understand them. It seemed to me that there must be a defect in the translation, and an erroneous exegesis; but where was the source of the error? I could not find it; and yet the error itself was very plain.

In opposition to the Mosaic law, which declares that if a man take an aversion to his wife he may write her a bill of divorcement and send her out of his house in opposition to this law Jesus is made to declare, "But I say unto you, That whosoever shall put away his wife, saving for the cause of fornication, causeth her to commit adultery." I saw nothing in these words to allow us to affirm that divorce was either permitted or forbidden. It is said that whoever shall put away his wife causes her to commit adultery, and then an exception is made with regard to a woman guilty of adultery. This exception, which throws the guilt of marital infidelity entirely upon the woman is, in general, strange and unexpected; but here, in relation to the context, it is simply absurd, for even the very doubtful meaning which might otherwise he attributed to it is wholly destroyed. Whoever puts away his wife exposes her to the crime of adultery, and yet a man is permitted to put away a wife guilty of adultery, as if a woman guilty of adultery would no more commit adultery after she were put away.

But this is not all; when I had examined this passage attentively, I found it also to be lacking in grammatical meaning. The words are, "Whoever shall put away his wife, except for the fault of adultery, exposes her to the commission of adultery," and the proposition is complete. It is a question of the husband, of him who in putting away his wife exposes her to the commission of the crime of adultery; what, then, is the purport of the qualifying phrase, "except for the fault of adultery"? If the proposition were in this form: Whoever shall put away his wife is guilty of adultery, unless the wife herself has been unfaithful it would be grammatically correct. But as the passage now stands, the subject "whoever" has no other predicate than the word "exposes," with which the phrase "except for the fault of adultery "cannot be connected. What, then, is the purport of this phrase? It is plain that whether for or without the fault of adultery on the part of the woman, the husband who puts away his wife exposes her to the commission of adultery.

The proposition is analogous to the following sentence: Whoever refuses food to his son, besides the fault of spitefulness, exposes him to the possibility of being cruel. This sentence evidently cannot mean that a father may refuse food to his son if the latter is spiteful. It can only mean that a father who refuses food to his son, besides being spiteful towards his son, exposes his son to the possibility of becoming cruel. And in the same way, the Gospel proposition would have a meaning if we could replace the words, "the fault of adultery," by libertinism, debauchery, or some similar phrase, expressing not an act but a quality.

And so I asked myself if the meaning here was not simply that whoever puts away his wife, besides being himself guilty of libertinism (since no one puts away his wife except to take another), exposes his wife to the commission of adultery? If, in the original text, the word translated "adultery" or "fornication" had the meaning of libertinism, the meaning of the passage would be clear. And then I met with the same experience that had happened to me before in similar instances. The text confirmed my suppositions and entirely effaced my doubts.

The first thing that occurred to me in reading the text was that the word πορνεια translated in common with μοιχασθαι, "adultery" or "fornication," is an entirely different word from the latter. But perhaps these two words are used as synonyms in the Gospels? I consulted the dictionary, and found that the word πορνεια, corresponding in Hebrew to *zanah*, in Latin to *fornication*, in German to *hurerei*, in French to *libertinage*, has a very precise meaning, and that it never has signified, and never can signify, the act of adultery, *Ehebruch*, as Luther and the Germans after him have rendered the word. It signifies a state of depravity, a quality, and not an act, and never can be properly translated by "adultery" or "fornication." I found, moreover, that "adultery" is expressed throughout the Gospel, as well as in the passage under consideration, by the word μοιχεω. I had only to correct the false translation, which had evidently been made intentionally, to render absolutely inadmissible the meaning attributed by commentators to the text, and to show the proper grammatical relation of πορνεια to the subject of the sentence.

A person acquainted with Greek would construe as follows: Παρεχτος, "except, outside," λογου, "the matter, the cause," πορνειας, "of libertinism," ποιει, "obliges," αυτην, "her," μοιχασθαι, "to be an adulteress" which rendering gives, word for

word, "Whoever puts away his wife, besides the fault of libertinism, obliges her to be an adulteress."

We obtain the same meaning from Matt. xix. 9. When we
correct the unauthorized translation of πορνεια, by substituting
"libertinism" for "fornication," we see at once that the phrase
ει μη επι πορνεια cannot apply to "wife." And as the words
παρεχτος λογου πορνειας could signify nothing else than the
fault of libertinism on the part of the husband, so the words ει
μη επι πορνεια, in the nineteenth chapter, can have no other
than the same meaning. The phrase ει μη επι πορνεια is, word
for word, "if this is not through libertinism" (to give one's self up
to libertinism). The meaning then becomes dear. Jesus replies to
the theory of the Pharisees, that a man who abandons his wife
to marry another with out the intention of giving himself up to
libertinism does not commit adultery Jesus replies to this theory
that the abandonment of a wife, that is, the cessation of sexual
relations, even if not for the purpose of libertinism, but to marry
another, is none the less adultery. Thus we come at the simple
meaning of this commandment a meaning which accords with
the whole doctrine, with the words of which it is the complement,
with grammar, and with logic. This simple and clear interpretation, harmonizing so naturally with the doctrine and the words
from which it was derived, I discovered after the most careful
and prolonged research. Upon a premeditated alteration of the
text had been based an exegesis which destroyed the moral, religious, logical, and grammatical meaning of Jesus words.

And thus once more I found a confirmation of the terrible fact
that the meaning of the doctrine of Jesus is simple and clear, that
its affirmations are emphatic and precise, but that commentaries upon the doctrine, inspired by a desire to sanction existing
evil, have so obscured it that determined effort is demanded of
him who would know the truth. If the Gospels had come down
to us in a fragmentary condition, it would have been easier (so
it seemed to me) to restore the true meaning of the text than to
find that meaning now, beneath the accumulations of fallacious
comments which have apparently no purpose save to conceal the
doctrine they are supposed to expound. With regard to the passage under consideration, it is plain that to justify the divorce of

some Byzantine emperor this ingenious pretext was employed to obscure the doctrine regulating the relations between the sexes. When we have rejected the suggestions of the commentators, we escape from the mist of uncertainty, and the second commandment of Jesus becomes precise and clear. "Guard against libertinism. Let every man justified in entering into the sexual relation have one wife, and every wife one husband, and under no pretext whatever let this union be violated by either."

Immediately after the second commandment is another reference to the ancient law, followed by the third commandment:

"Again, ye have heard that it hath been said by them of old time, Thou shalt not forswear thyself, but shalt perform unto the Lord thine oaths: But I say unto you, Swear not at all; neither by heaven; for it is God's throne: Nor by the earth; for it is his foot stool: neither by Jerusalem; for it is the city of the great King. Neither shalt thou swear by thy head, because thou canst not make one hair white or black. But let your communications be, Yea, yea; nay, nay: for whatsoever is more than these cometh of evil." (Matt. v. 33–37.)

This passage always troubled me when I read it. It did not trouble me by its obscurity, like the passage about divorce; or by conflicting with other passages, like the authorization of anger for cause; or by the difficulty in the way of obedience, as in the case of the command to turn the other cheek; it troubled me rather by its very clearness, simplicity, and practicality. Side by side with rules whose magnitude and importance I felt profoundly, was this saying, which seemed to me superfluous, frivolous, weak, and without consequence to me or to others. I naturally did not swear, either by Jerusalem, or by heaven, or by anything else, and it cost me not the least effort to refrain from doing so; on the other hand, it seemed to me that whether I swore or did not swear could not be of the slightest importance to anyone. And desiring to find an explanation of this rule, which troubled me through its very simplicity, I consulted the commentators. They were in this case of great assistance to me.

The commentators all found in these words a confirmation of the third commandment of Moses, not to swear by the name of the Lord; but, in addition to this, they explained that this commandment of Jesus against an oath was not always obligatory, and had no reference whatever to the oath which citizens are obliged to take before the authorities. And they brought together Scripture citations, not to support the direct meaning of Jesus commandment, but to prove when it ought and ought not to be obeyed. They claimed that Jesus had himself sanctioned the oath in courts of justice by his reply, *"Thou hast said,"* to the words of the High Priest, *"I adjure thee by the living God;"* that the apostle Paul invoked God to witness the truth of his words, which invocation was evidently equivalent to an oath; that the law of Moses proscribing the oath was not abrogated by Jesus; and that Jesus forbade only false oaths, the oaths of Pharisees and hypocrites. When I had read these comments, I under stood that unless I excepted from the oaths forbid den by Jesus the oath of fidelity to the State, the commandment was as insignificant as superficial, and as easy to practise as I had supposed.

And I asked myself the question; does this passage contain an exhortation to abstain from an oath that the commentators of the Church are so zealous to justify? Does it not forbid us to take the oath indispensable to the assembling of men into political groups and the formation of a military caste? The soldier, that special instrument of violence, goes in Russia by the nickname of *prissaiaga* (sworn in). If I had asked the soldier at the Borovitzky Gate how he solved the contradiction between the Gospels and military regulations, he would have replied that he had taken the oath, that is, that he had sworn by the Gospels. This is the reply that soldiers always make. The oath is so indispensable to the horrors of war and armed coercion that in France, where Christianity is out of favor, the oath remains in full force. If Jesus did not say in so many words, "Do not take an oath," the prohibition ought to be a consequence of his teaching. He came to suppress evil, and, if he did not condemn the oath, he left a terrible evil untouched. It may be said, perhaps, that at the time at which Jesus lived this evil passed unperceived; but this is not true. Epictetus and Seneca declare against the taking of oaths. A similar rule is inscribed in the *Laws of Manu*. The Jews of the time of Jesus made proselytes, and obliged them to take the oath. How could it be said that Jesus did not perceive this evil when he forbade it in clear, direct, and circumstantial terms? He said, *"Swear not at all."* This expression is as simple, clear, and absolute as the expression, *"Judge not, condemn not,"* and is as little subject to explanation; moreover, he added to this, *"Let your communication be, Yea, yea; Nay, nay: for whatsoever is more than these cometh of evil."*

If obedience to the doctrine of Jesus consists in perpetual observance of the will of God, how can a man swear to observe the will of another man or other men? The will of God cannot coincide with the will of man. And this is precisely what Jesus said in Matt. v. 36:

"Neither shalt thou swear by thy head, because thou canst not make one hair white or black."

And the apostle James says in his epistle, v. 12:

"But above all things, my brethren, swear not, neither by heaven, neither by earth, neither by any other oath: but let your yea be yea; and your nay, nay; lest ye fall into condemnation."

The apostle tells us clearly why we must not swear: the oath in itself may be unimportant, but by it men are condemned, and so we ought not to swear at all. How could we express more clearly the saying of Jesus and his apostle?

My ideas had become so confused that for a long time I had kept before me the question, do the words and the meaning of this passage agree? It does not seem possible. But, after having read the commentaries attentively, I saw that the impossible had become a fact. The explanations of the commentators were in harmony with those they had offered concerning the other commandments of Jesus: judge not, be not angry, do not violate the marital bonds.

We have organized a social order which we cherish and look upon as sacred. Jesus, whom we recognize as God, comes and tells us that our social organization is wrong. We recognize him as God, but we are not willing to renounce our social institutions. What, then, are we to do? Add, if we can, the words "without a cause" to render void the command against anger; mutilate the sense of another law, as audacious prevaricators have done by substituting for the command absolutely forbidding divorce, phraseology which permits divorce; and if there is no possible way of deriving an equivocal meaning, as in the case of the commands, *"Judge not, condemn not"* and *"Swear not at all"* then with the utmost effrontery openly violate the rule while affirming that we obey it.

In fact, the principal obstacle to a comprehension of the truth that the Gospel forbids all manner of oaths exists in the fact that our pseudo-Christian commentators themselves, with unexampled audacity, take oath upon the Gospel itself. They make men swear by the Gospel, that is to say, they do just the contrary of what the Gospel commands. Why does it never occur to the man who is made to take an oath upon the cross and the Gospel that the cross was made sacred only by the death of one who forbade all oaths, and that in kissing the sacred book he perhaps is pressing his lips upon the very page where is recorded the clear and direct commandment, *"Swear not at all"*?

But I was troubled no more with regard to the meaning of the passage comprised in Matt. v. 33–37 when I found the plain declaration of the third commandment, that we should take no oath, since all oaths are imposed for an evil purpose.

After the third commandment comes the fourth reference to the ancient law and the enunciation of the fourth commandment:

"Ye have heard that it hath been said, An eye for an eye, and a tooth for a tooth: But I say unto you, That ye resist not evil: but whosoever shall smite thee on thy right cheek, turn to him the other also. And if any man will sue thee at the law, and take away thy coat, let him have thy cloak also. And whosoever shall compel thee to go a mile, go with him twain. Give to him that asketh thee, and from him that would borrow of thee turn not thou away." (*Matt. v. 38–12.*)

I have already spoken of the direct and precise meaning of these words; I have already said that we have no reason whatever for basing upon them an allegorical explanation. The comments that have been made upon them, from the time of Chrysostom to our day, are really surprising. The words are pleasing to everyone, and they inspire all manner of profound reflections save one, that these words express exactly what Jesus meant to say. The Church commentators, not at all awed by the authority of one whom they recognize as God, boldly distort the meaning of his words. They tell us, of course, that these commandments to bear offences and to refrain from reprisals are directed against the vindictive character of the Jews; they not only do not exclude all general measures for the repression of evil and the punishment of evildoers, but they exhort every one to individual and personal effort to sustain justice, to apprehend aggressors, and to prevent the wicked from inflicting evil upon others, for, otherwise (they tell us) these spiritual commandments of the Saviour would be come, as they became among the Jews, a dead letter, and would serve only to propagate evil and to sup press virtue. The love of the Christian should be patterned after the love of God; but divine love circumscribes and reproves evil only as may be required for the glory of God and the safety of his servants, If evil is propagated, we must set bounds to evil and punish it, now this is the duty of authorities.

Christian scholars and free-thinkers are not embarrassed by the meaning of these words of Jesus, and do not hesitate to correct them. The sentiments here expressed, they tell us, are very noble, but are completely inapplicable to life; for if we practised to the letter the commandment, "Resist not evil" our entire social fabric would be destroyed. This is what Renan, Strauss, and all the liberal commentators tell us. If, however, we take the words of Jesus as we would take the words of anyone who speaks to us, and admit that he says exactly what he does say, all these profound circumlocutions vanish away. Jesus says, "Your social system is absurd and wrong. I propose to you another." And then he utters the teachings reported by Matthew (v. 38–42). It would seem that before correcting them one ought to understand them; now this is exactly what no one wishes to do. We decide in advance that the social order which controls our existence, and which is abolished by these words, is the superior law of humanity.

For my part, I consider our social order to be neither wise nor sacred; and that is why I have understood this commandment when others have not. And when I had understood these words just as they are written, I was struck with their truth, their lucidity, and their precision. Jesus said, "You wish to suppress evil by evil; this is not reasonable. To abolish evil, avoid the commission of evil." And then he enumerates instances where we are in the habit of returning evil for evil, and says that in these cases we ought not so to do.

This fourth commandment was the one that I first understood; and it revealed to me the meaning of all the others. This simple, clear, and practical fourth commandment says: "Never resist evil by force, never return violence for violence: if anyone beat you, bear it; if one would deprive you of anything, yield to his wishes; if anyone would force you to labor, labor; if anyone would take away your property, abandon it at his demand."

After the fourth commandment we find a fifth reference to the ancient law, followed by the fifth commandment:

"Ye have heard that it hath been said, Thou shalt love thy neighbor and hate thine enemy. But I say unto you, Love your enemies, bless them that curse you, do good to them that hate you, and pray for them which despitefully use you, and persecute you; That ye may be the children of your Father which is in heaven: for he maketh his sun to rise on the evil and on the good, and sendeth rain on the just and on the unjust. For if ye love them which love you, what reward have ye? Do not even the publicans the same? And if ye salute your brethren only, what do ye more than others? Do not even the publicans so? He ye therefore perfect, even as your Father which is in heaven is perfect." (Matt. v. 43–48.)

These verses I had formerly regarded as a continuation, an exposition, an enforcement, I might almost say an exaggeration, of the words, *"Resist not evil."* But as I had found a simple, precise, and practical meaning in each of the passages beginning with a reference to the ancient law, I anticipated a similar experience here. After each reference of this sort had thus far come a commandment, and each commandment had been important and distinct in meaning; it ought to be so now. The closing words of the passage, repeated by Luke, which are to the effect that God makes no distinction of persons, but lavishes his gifts upon all, and that we, following his precepts, ought to regard all men as equally worthy, and to do good to all, these words were clear; they seemed to me to be a confirmation and exposition of some definite law but what was this law? For a long time I could not understand it.

To love one's enemies? This was impossible. It was one of those sublime thoughts that we must look upon only as an indication of a moral ideal impossible of attainment. It demanded all or nothing. We might, perhaps, refrain from doing injury to our enemies but to love them! No; Jesus did not command the impossible. And besides, in the words referring to the ancient law, "*Ye have heard that it hath been said, Thou shalt . . . hate thine enemy,*" there was cause for doubt. In other references Jesus cited textually the terms of the Mosaic law; but here he apparently cites words that have no such authority; he seems to calumniate the Law of Moses.

As with regard to my former doubts, so now the commentators gave me no explanation of the difficulty. They all agreed that the words "hate thine enemy" were not in the Mosaic law, but the offered no suggestion as to the meaning of the unauthorized phrase. They spoke of the difficulty of loving one's enemies, that is, wicked men (thus they amended Jesus words); and they said that while it is impossible to love our enemies, we may refrain from wishing them harm and from inflicting injury upon them. Moreover, they insinuated that we might and should "convince" our enemies, that is, resist them; they spoke of the different degrees of love for our enemies which we might attain from all of which the final conclusion was that Jesus, for some inexplicable reason, quoted as from the law of Moses words not to be found therein, and then uttered a number of sublime phrases which at bottom are impracticable and empty of meaning.

I could not agree with this conclusion. In this passage, as in the passages containing the first four commandments, there must be some clear and precise meaning. To find this meaning, I set myself first of all to discover the purport of the words containing the inexact reference to the ancient law, "*Ye have, heard that it hath been said, Thou shalt hate thine enemy.*" Jesus had some reason for placing at the head of each of his commandments certain portions of the ancient law to serve as the antitheses of his own doctrine. If we do not understand what is meant by the citations from the ancient law, we cannot understand what Jesus proscribed. The commentators say frankly (it is impossible not to say so) that Jesus in this instance made use of words not to be found in the Mosaic law, but they do not tell us why he did so or what meaning we are to attach to the words thus used.

It seemed to me above all necessary to know what Jesus had in view when he cited these words which are not to be found in the law. I asked myself what these words could mean. In all other references of the sort, Jesus quotes a single rule from the ancient law: "Thou shalt not kill" "Thou shalt not commit adultery" "Thou shalt not forswear thyself" "An eye for an eye, a tooth for a tooth" and with regard to each rule he propounds his own doctrine. In the instance under consideration, he cites two contrasting rules: *"Ye have heard that it hath been said, Thou shalt love thy neighbor and hate thine enemy,"* from which it would appear that the contrast between these two rules of the ancient law, relative to one's neighbor and one's enemy, should be the basis of the new law. To understand clearly what this contrast was, I sought for the meanings of the words "neighbor" and "enemy," as used in the Gospel text. After consulting dictionaries and Biblical texts, I was convinced that "neighbor" in the Hebrew language meant, invariably and exclusively, a Hebrew. We find the same meaning expressed in the Gospel parable of the Samaritan. From the inquiry of the Jewish scribe (Luke x. 29), "And who is my neighbor?" it is plain that he did not regard the Samaritan as such. The word "neighbor" is used with the same meaning in Acts vii. 27. "Neighbor," in Gospel language, means a compatriot, a person belonging to the same nationality. And so the antithesis used by Jesus in the citation, "love thy neighbor, hate thine enemy," must be in the distinction between the words "compatriot" and "foreigner." I then sought for the Jewish understanding of "enemy," and I found my supposition confirmed. The word "enemy" is nearly always employed in the Gospels in the sense, not of a personal enemy, but, in general, of a "hostile people" (Luke i. 71, 74; Matt. xxii; Mark xii. 36; Luke xx. 43, etc.). The use of the word "enemy" in the singular form, in the phrase "hate thine enemy," convinced me that the meaning is a "hostile people." In the Old Testament, the conception "hostile people" is nearly always expressed in the singular form.

When I understood this, I understood why Jesus, who had before quoted the authentic words of the law, had here cited the words "*hate thine enemy.*" When we understand the word "enemy "in the sense of "hostile people," and "neighbor" in the sense of "compatriot," the difficulty is completely solved. Jesus spoke of the manner in which Moses directed the Hebrews to act toward "hostile peoples." The various passages scattered through the different books of the Old Testament, prescribing the oppression, slaughter, and extermination of other peoples, Jesus summed up in one word, "hate," make war upon the enemy. He said, in substance: "You have heard that you must love those of your own race, and hate foreigners; but I say unto you, love every one without distinction of nationality." When I had understood these words in this way, I saw immediately the force of the phrase, "Love your enemies" It is impossible to love one's personal enemies; but it is perfectly possible to love the citizens of a foreign nation equally with one's compatriots. And I saw clearly that in saying, "Ye have heard that it hath been said, Thou shalt love thy neighbor, and hate thine enemy. But I say unto you, Love your enemies" Jesus meant to say that men are in the habit of looking upon compatriots as neighbors, and foreigners as enemies; and this he reproved. His meaning was that the Law of Moses established a difference between the Hebrew and the foreigner the hostile peoples; but he forbade any such difference. And then, according to Matthew and Luke, after giving this commandment, he said that with God all men are equal, all are warmed by the same sun, all profit by the same rain. God makes no distinction among peoples, and lavishes his gifts upon all men; men ought to act exactly in the same way toward one another, without distinction of nationality, and not like the heathen, who divide themselves into distinct nationalities.

Thus once more I found confirmed on all sides the simple, clear, important, and practical meaning of the words of Jesus. Once more, in place of an obscure sentence, I had found a clear, precise, important, and practical rule: To make no distinction between compatriots and foreigners, and to abstain from all the results of such distinction, from hostility towards foreigners, from wars, from all participation in war, from all preparations for war; to establish with all men, of whatever nationality, the same relations granted to compatriots. All this was so simple and so clear, that I was Astonished that I had not perceived it from the first.

The cause of my error was the same as that which had perplexed me with regard to the passages relating to judgments and the taking of oaths. It is very difficult to believe that tribunals upheld by professed Christians, blest by those who consider themselves the guardians of the law of Jesus, could be incompatible with the Christian religion; could be, in fact, diametrically opposed to it. It is still more difficult to believe that the oath which we are obliged to take by the guardians of the law of Jesus, is directly reproved by this law. To admit that everything in life that is considered essential and natural, as well as what is considered the most noble and grand, love of country, its defence, its glory, battle with its enemies, to admit that all this is not only an infraction of the law of Jesus, but is directly denounced by Jesus, this, I say, is difficult.

Our existence is now so entirely in contradiction with the doctrine of Jesus, that only with the greatest difficulty can we understand its meaning. We have been so deaf to the rules of life that he has given us, to his explanations, not only when he commands us not to kill, but when he warns us against anger, when he commands us not to resist evil, to turn the other cheek, to love our enemies; we are so accustomed to speak of a body of men especially organized for murder, as a Christian army, we are so accustomed to prayers addressed to the Christ for the assurance of victory, we who have, made the sword, that symbol of murder, an almost sacred object (so that a man deprived of this symbol, of his sword, is a dishonored man); we are so accustomed, I say, to this, that the words of Jesus seem to us compatible with war. We say, "If he had forbidden it, he would have said so plainly." We forget that Jesus did not foresee that men having faith in his doctrine of humility, love, and fraternity, could ever, with calmness and premeditation, organize themselves for the murder of their brethren.

Jesus did not foresee this, and so he did not forbid a Christian to participate in war. A father who exhorts his son to live honestly, never to wrong any person, and to give all that he has to others, would not forbid his son to kill people upon the highway.

None of the apostles, no disciple of Jesus during the first centuries of Christianity, realized the necessity of forbidding a Christian that form of murder which we call war.

Here, for example, is what Origen says in his reply to Celsus:

"In the next place, Celsus urges us 'to help the king with all our might, and to labor with him in the maintenance of justice, to fight for him; and,' if he requires it, to fight under him, or lead an army along with him. To this, our answer is that we do, when occasion requires, give help to kings, and that, so to say, a divine help, 'putting on the whole armour of God.' And this we do in obedience to the injunction of the apostle, I exhort, therefore, that first of all, supplications, prayers, intercessions, and giving of thanks, be made for all men, for kings, and for all that are in authority; and the more anyone excels in piety, the more effective help does he render to kings, even more than is given by soldiers, who go forth to fight and slay as many of the enemy as they can. And to those enemies of our faith who require us to bear arms for the common wealth, and to slay men, we can reply: 'Do not those who are priests at certain shrines, and those who attend on certain gods, as you account them, keep their hands free from blood, that they may with hands unstained and free from human blood, offer the appointed sacrifices to your gods? And even when war is upon you, you never enlist the priests in the army. If that, then, is a laudable custom, how much more so, that while others are engaged in battle, these too should engage as the priests and ministers of God, keeping their hands pure, and wrestling in prayers to God on behalf of those who are fighting in a righteous cause, and for the king who reigns righteously, that whatever is opposed to those who act righteously may be destroyed! "

And at the close of the chapter, in explaining that Christians, through their peaceful lives, are much more helpful to kings than soldiers are, Origen says:

"And none fight better for the king than we do. We do not, indeed, fight under him, although he require it; but we fight on his behalf, forming a special army, an army of piety, by offering our prayers to God."

This is the way in which the Christians of the first centuries regarded war, and such was the language that their leaders addressed to the rulers of the earth at a period when martyrs perished by hundreds and by thousands for having confessed the religion of Jesus, the Christ.

And now is not the question settled as to whether a Christian may or may not go to war? All young men brought up according to the doctrine of the Church called Christian, are obliged at a specified date during every autumn, to report at the bureaus of conscription and, under the guidance of their spiritual directors, deliberately to renounce the religion of Jesus, Not long ago, there was a peasant who refused military service on the plea that it was contrary to the Gospel. The doctors of the Church explained to the peasant his error; but, as the peasant had faith, not in their words, but in those of Jesus, he was thrown into prison, where he remained until he was ready to renounce the law of Christ. And all this happened after Christians had heard for eighteen hundred years the clear, precise, and practical commandment of their Master, which teaches not to consider men of different nationality as enemies, but to consider all men as brethren, and to maintain with them the same relations existing among compatriots; to refrain not only from killing those who are called enemies, but to love them and to minister to their needs.

When I had understood these simple and precise commandments of Jesus, these commandments so ill adapted to the ingenious distortions of commentators, I asked myself what would be the result if the whole Christian world believed in them, believed not only in reading and chanting them for the glory of God, but also in obeying them for the good of humanity? What would be the result if men believed in the observance of these commandments at least as seriously as they believe in daily devotions, in attendance on Sunday worship, in weekly fasts, in the holy sacrament? What would be the result if the faith of men in these commandments were as strong as their faith in the requirements of the Church? And then I saw in imagination a Christian society living according to these commandments and educating the younger generation to follow their precepts. I tried to picture the results if we taught our children from infancy, not what we teach them now to maintain personal dignity, to uphold personal privileges against the encroachments of others (which we can never do without humiliating or offending others) but to teach them that no man has a right to privileges, and can neither be above or below anyone else; that he alone debases and demeans himself who tries to domineer over others; that a man can be in a no more contemptible condition than when he is angry with another; that what may seem to be foolish and despicable in another is no excuse for wrath or enmity. I sought to imagine the results if, instead of extolling our social organization as it now is, with its theatres, its romances, its sumptuous methods for stimulating sensuous desires if, instead of this, we taught our children by precept and by example, that the reading of lascivious romances and attendance at theatres and balls are the most vulgar of all distractions, and that there is nothing more grotesque and humiliating than to pass one's time in the collection and arrangement of personal finery to make of one's body an object of show. I endeavored to imagine a state of society (where, instead of permitting and approving libertinism in young men before marriage, instead of regarding the separation of husband and wife as natural and desirable, instead of giving to women the legal right to practise the trade of prostitution, instead of countenancing and sanctioning divorce if, instead of this, we taught by words and actions that the state of celibacy, the solitary existence of a man properly endowed for, and who has not renounced the sexual relation, is a monstrous and opprobrious wrong; and that the abandonment of wife by husband or of husband by wife for the sake of another, is an act against nature, an act bestial and inhuman.

Instead of regarding it as natural that our entire existence should be controlled by coercion; that every one of our amusements should be provided and maintained by force; that each of us from childhood to old age should be by turns victim and executioner instead of this I tried to picture the results if, by precept and example, we endeavored to inspire the world with the conviction that vengeance is a sentiment unworthy of humanity; that violence is not only debasing, but that it deprives us of all capacity for happiness; that the true pleasures of life are not those maintained by force; and that our greatest consideration ought to be bestowed, not upon those who accumulate riches to the injury of others, but upon those who best serve others and give what they have to lessen the woes of their kind. If instead of regarding the taking of an oath and the placing of ourselves and our lives at the disposition of another as a rightful and praiseworthy act, I tried to imagine what would be the result if we taught that the enlightened will of man is alone sacred; and that if a man place himself at the disposition of anyone, and promise by oath anything whatever, he renounces his rational manhood and outrages his most sacred right. I tried to imagine the results, if, instead of the national hatred with which we are inspired under the name of "patriotism"; if, in place of the glory associated with that form of murder which we call war, if, in place of this, we were taught, on the contrary, horror and contempt for all the means military, diplomatic, and political which serve to divide men; if we were educated to look upon the division of men into political States, and a diversity of codes and frontiers, as an indication of barbarism; and that to massacre others is a most horrible crime, only to be perpetrated by a depraved and misguided man, who has fallen to the lowest level of the brute. I imagined that all men had arrived at these convictions, and I considered what I thought would be the result.

Up to this time (I said), what have been the practical results of the doctrine of Jesus, as I understand it? And the involuntary reply was, nothing. "We continue to pray, to partake of the sacraments, to believe in the redemption, and in our personal salvation as well as that of the world by Jesus the Christ, and yet hold that salvation will never come by our efforts, but will come because the period set for the end of the world will have arrived when the Christ will appear in his glory to judge the quick and the dead, and the kingdom of heaven will be established.

Now the doctrine of Jesus, as I understood it, had an entirely different meaning. The establishment of the kingdom of God depended upon our personal efforts in the practice of Jesus doctrine as propounded in the five commandments, which instituted the kingdom of God upon earth. The kingdom of God upon earth consists in this that all men should be at peace with one another. It was thus that the Hebrew prophets conceived of the rule of God. Peace among men is the greatest blessing that can exist upon this earth, and it is within reach of all men. This ideal is in every human heart. The prophets all brought to men the promise of peace. The whole doctrine of Jesus has but one object, to establish peace the kingdom of God among men.

In the Sermon on the Mount, in the interview with Nicodemus, in the instructions given to his disciples, in all his teachings, Jesus spoke only of this, of the things that divided men, that kept them from peace that prevented them from entering into the kingdom of heaven. The parables make clear to us what the kingdom of heaven is, and show us the only way of entering therein, which is to love our brethren, and to be at peace with all. John the Baptist, the forerunner of Jesus, proclaimed the approach of the kingdom of God, and declared that Jesus was to bring it upon earth. Jesus himself said that his mission was to bring peace:

"Peace I leave with you, my peace I give unto you: not as the world giveth, give I unto you. Let not your heart be troubled, neither let it be afraid" (John xiv. 27).

And the observance of his five commandments will bring peace upon the earth. They all have but one object, the establishment of peace among men. If men will only believe in the doctrine of Jesus and practise it, the reign of peace will come upon earth, not that peace which is the work of man, partial, precarious, and at the mercy of chance; but the peace that is all-pervading, inviolable, and eternal.

The first commandment tells us to be at peace with every one and to consider none as foolish or unworthy. If peace is violated, we are to seek to re-establish it. The true religion is in the extinction of enmity among men. We are to be reconciled without delay, that we may not lose that inner peace which is the true life (Matt. v. 22–24). Everything is comprised in this commandment; but Jesus knew the worldly temptations that prevent peace among men. The first temptation perilous to peace is that of the sexual relation. We are not to consider the body as an instrument of lust; each man is to have one wife, and each woman one husband, and one is never to forsake the other under any pretext (Matt. v. 28–32). The second temptation is that of the oath, which draws men into sin; this is wrong, and we are not to be bound by any such promise (Matt, v. 34–37). The third temptation is that of vengeance, which we call human justice; this we are not to resort to under any pretext; we are to endure offences and never to return evil for evil (Matt. v. 38–42). The fourth temptation is that arising from difference in nationalities, from hostility between peoples and States; but we are to remember that all men are brothers, and children of the same Father, and thus take care that difference in nationality leads not to the destruction of peace (Matt. v. 43–48).

If men abstain from practising anyone of these commandments, peace will be violated. Let men practise all these commandments, which exclude evil from the lives of men, and peace will be established upon earth. The practice of these five commandments would realize the ideal of human life existing in every human heart. All men would be brothers; each would be at peace with others, enjoying all the blessings of earth to the limit of years accorded by the Creator. Men would beat their swords into plough-shares, and their spears into priming hooks, and then would come the kingdom of God, that reign of peace foretold by all the prophets, which was foretold by John the Baptist as near at hand, and which Jesus proclaimed in the words of Isaiah:

"The Spirit of the Lord is upon me, because he hath anointed me to preach the gospel to the poor; he hath sent me to heal the broken hearted, to preach deliverance to the captives, and recovering of sight to the blind, to set at liberty them that are bruised, to preach the acceptable year of the Lord. And he began to say unto them, Today hath this Scripture been fulfilled in your ears" (Luke iv. 18, 19, 21).

The commandments for peace given by Jesus, those simple and clear commandments, foreseeing all possibilities of discussion, and anticipating all objections, these commandments proclaimed the kingdom of God upon earth. Jesus, then, was, in truth, the Messiah. He fulfilled what had been promised. But we have not fulfilled the commands we must fulfil if the kingdom of God is to be established upon earth, that kingdom which men in all ages have earnestly desired, and have sought for continually, all their days.

Chapter 7

WHY IS IT THAT MEN have not done as Jesus commanded them, and thus secured the greatest happiness within their reach, the happiness they have always longed for and still desire? The reply to this inquiry is always the same, although expressed in different ways. The doctrine of Jesus (we are told) is admirable, and it is true that if we practised it, we should see the kingdom of God established upon earth; but to practise it is difficult, and consequently this doctrine is impracticable. The doctrine of Jesus, which teaches men how they should live, is admirable, is divine; it brings true happiness, but it is difficult to practise. We repeat this, and hear it repeated so many, many times, that we do not observe the contradiction contained in these words.

It is natural to each human being to do what seems to him best. Any doctrine teaching men how they should live instructs them only as to what is best for each. If we show men what they have to do to attain what is best for each, how can they say that they would like to do it, but that it is impossible of attainment? According to the law of their nature they cannot do what is worse for each, and yet they declare that they cannot do what is best.

The reasonable activity of man, from his earliest existence, has been applied to the search for what is best among the contradictions that envelop human life. Men struggled for the soil, for objects which are necessary to them; then they arrived at the division of goods, and called this property; finding that this arrangement, although difficult to establish, was best, they maintained ownership. Men fought with one another for the possession of women, they abandoned their children; then they found it was best that each should have his own family; and although it was difficult to sustain a family, they maintained the family, as they did ownership and many other things. As soon as they discover that a thing is best, however difficult of attainment, men do it. What, then, is the meaning of the saying that the doctrine of Jesus is admirable, that a life according to the doctrine of Jesus would be better than the life which men now lead, but that men cannot lead this better life because it is difficult?

If the word "difficult," used in this way, is to be understood in the sense that it is difficult to renounce the fleeting satisfaction of sensual desires that we may obtain a greater good, why do we not say that it is difficult to labor for bread, difficult to plant a tree that we may enjoy the fruit? Every being endowed with even the most rudimentary reason knows that he must endure difficulties to procure any good, superior to that which he has enjoyed before. And yet we say that the doctrine of Jesus is admirable, but impossible of practice, because it is difficult! Now it is difficult, because in following it we are obliged to deprive ourselves of many things that we have hitherto enjoyed. Have we never heard that it is far more to our advantage to endure difficulties and privations than to satisfy all our desires? Man may fall to the level of the beasts, but he ought not to make use of his reason to devise an apology for his bestiality. From the moment that he begins to reason, he is conscious of being endowed with reason, and this consciousness stimulates him to distinguish between the reasonable and the unreasonable. Reason does not proscribe; it enlightens.

Suppose that I am shut into a dark room, and in searching for the door I continually bruise myself against the walls. Someone brings me a light, and I see the door. I ought no longer to bruise myself when I see the door; much less ought I to affirm that, although it is best to go out through the door, it is difficult to do so, and that, consequently, I prefer to bruise myself against the walls.

In this marvellous argument that the doctrine of Jesus is admirable, and that its practice would give the world true happiness, but that men are weak and sinful, that they would do the best and do the worst, and so cannot do the best, in this strange plea there is an evident misapprehension; there is something else besides defective reasoning; there is also a chimerical idea. Only a chimerical idea, mistaking reality for what does not exist, and taking the non-existent for reality, could lead men to deny the possibility of practising that which by their own avowal would be for their true welfare.

The chimerical idea which has reduced men to this condition is that of the dogmatic Christian religion, as it is taught through the various catechisms, to all who profess the Christianity of the Church. This religion, according to the definition of it given by its followers, consists in accepting as real that which does not exist these are Paul's words, and they are repeated in all the theologies and catechisms as the best definition of faith. It is this faith in the reality of what does not exist that leads men to make the strange affirmation that the doctrine of Jesus is excellent for all men, but is worth nothing as a guide to their way of living. Here is an exact summary of what this religion teaches:

A personal God, who is from all eternity one of three persons decided to create a world of spirits. This God of goodness created the world of spirits for their own happiness, but it so happened that one of the spirits became spontaneously wicked. Time passed, and God created a material world, created man for man's own happiness, created man happy, immortal, and without sin. The felicity of man consisted in the enjoyment of life without toil; his immortality was due to the promise that this life should last forever; his innocence was due to the fact that he had no conception of evil.

Man was beguiled in paradise by one of the spirits of the first creation, who had become spontaneously wicked. From this dates the fall of man, who engendered other men fallen like himself, and from this time men have endured toil, sickness, suffering, death, the physical and moral struggle for existence; that is to say, the fantastic being pre ceding the fall became real, as we know him to be, as we have no right or reason to imagine him not to be. The state of man who toils, who suffers, who chooses what is for his own welfare and rejects what would be injurious to him, who dies, this state, which is the real and only conceivable state, is not, according to the doctrine of this religion, the normal state of man, but a state which is unnatural and temporary.

Although this state, according to the doctrine, has lasted for all humanity since the expulsion of Adam from paradise, that is, from the commencement of the world until the birth of Jesus, and has continued since the birth of Jesus under exactly the same conditions, the faithful are asked to believe that this is an abnormal and temporary state. According to this doctrine, the Son of God, the second person of the Trinity, who was himself God, was sent by God into the world in the garb of humanity to rescue men from this temporary and abnormal state; to deliver them from the pains with which they had been stricken by this same God because of Adam's sin; and to restore them to their former normal state of felicity, that is to immortality, innocence, and idleness. The second person of the Trinity (according to this doctrine), by suffering death at the hands of man, atoned for Adam's sin, and put an end to that abnormal state which had lasted from the commencement of the world. And from that time onward, the men who have had faith in Jesus have returned to the state of the first man in paradise; that is, have become immortal, innocent, and idle.

The doctrine does not concern itself too closely with the practical result of the redemption, in virtue of which the earth after Jesus coming ought to have become once more, at least for believers, everywhere fertile, without need of human toil; sickness ought to have ceased, and mothers have borne children without pain; since it is difficult to assure even believers who are worn by excessive labor and broken down by suffering, that toil is light, and suffering easy to endure.

But that portion of the doctrine which proclaims the abrogation of death and of sin, is affirmed with redoubled emphasis. It is asserted that the dead continue to live. And as the dead cannot bear witness that they are dead or prove that they are living (just as a stone is unable to affirm either that it can or cannot speak), this absence of denial is admitted as proof, and it is affirmed that dead men are not dead. It is affirmed with still more solemnity and assurance that, since the coming of Jesus, the man who has faith in him is free from sin; that is, that since the coming of Jesus, it is no longer necessary that man should guide his life by reason, and choose what is best for himself. He has only to believe that Jesus has redeemed his sins and he then becomes infallible, that is, perfect. According to this doctrine, men ought to believe that reason is powerless, and that for this cause they are without sin, that is, cannot err. A faithful believer ought to be convinced that since the coming of Jesus, the earth brings forth without labor, that childbirth no longer entails suffering, that diseases no longer exist, and that death and sin, that is, error, are destroyed; in a word, that what is, is not, and what is not, is.

Such is the rigorously logical theory of Christian theology. This doctrine, by itself, seems to be innocent. But deviations from truth are never inoffensive, and the significance of their consequences is in proportion to the importance of the subject to which these errors are applied. And here the subject at issue is the whole life of man. What this doctrine calls the true life, is a life of personal happiness, without sin, and eternal; that is, a life that no one has ever known, and which does not exist. But the life that is, the only life that we know, the life that we live and that all humanity lives and has lived, is, according to this doctrine, a degraded and evil existence, a mere phantasmagoria of the happy life which is our due.

Of the struggle between animal instincts and reason, which is the essence of human life, this doctrine takes no account. The struggle that Adam underwent in paradise, in deciding whether to eat or not to eat the fruit of the tree of knowledge, is according to this doctrine, no longer within the range of human experience. The question was decided, once for all, by Adam in paradise. Adam sinned for all; in other words, he did wrong, arid all men are irretrievably degraded; and all our efforts to live by reason are vain and even impious. This I ought to know, for I am irreparably bad. My salvation does not depend upon living by the light of reason, and, after distinguishing between good and evil, choosing the good; no, Adam, once for all, sinned for me, and Jesus, once for all, has atoned for the wrong committed by Adam; and so I ought, as a looker-on, to mourn over the fall of Adam and rejoice at the redemption through Jesus.

All the love for truth and goodness in the heart of man, all his efforts to illuminate his spiritual life by the light of reason, are not only of slight importance, according to this doctrine; they are a temptation, an incitement to pride. Life as it is upon this earth, with all its joys and its splendors, its struggles of reason with darkness, the life of all men that have lived before me, my own life with its inner struggles and triumphs, all this is not the true life; it is the fallen life, a life irretrievably bad. The true life, the life without sin, is only in faith, that is, in imagination, that is, in lunacy.

Let anyone break the habit contracted from infancy of believing this; let him look boldly at this doctrine as it is; let him endeavor to put himself in the position of a man without prejudice, educated independently of this doctrine and then let him ask himself if this doctrine would not appear to such a man as a product of absolute insanity.

However strange and shocking all this might appear to me, I was obliged to examine into it, for here alone I found the explanation of the objection, so devoid of logic and common sense, that I heard everywhere with regard to the impossibility of practising the doctrine of Jesus: It is admirable, and would give true happiness to men, but men are not able to obey it.

Only a conviction that reality does not exist, and that the nonexistent is real, could lead men to this surprising contradiction. And this false conviction I found in the pseudo-Christian religion which men had been teaching for fifteen hundred years.

The objection that the doctrine of Jesus is excellent but impracticable, comes not only from believers, but from sceptics, from those who do not believe, or think that they do not believe, in the dogmas of the fall of man and the redemption; from men of science and philosophers who consider themselves free from all prejudice. They believe, or imagine that they believe in nothing, and so consider them selves as above such a superstition as the dogma of the full and the redemption. At first it seemed to me that all such persona had serious motives for denying the possibility of practising the doctrine of Jesus. But when I came to look into the source of their negation, I was convinced that the sceptics, in common with the believers, have a false conception of life; to them life is not what it is, but what they imagine it ought to be, and this conception rests upon the same foundation as does that of the believers. It is true that the sceptics, who pretend to believe in nothing, believe not in God, or in Jesus, or in Adam; but they believe in a fundamental idea which is at the basis of their misconception, in the rights of man to a life of happiness, much more firmly than do the theologians.

In vain do science and philosophy pose as the arbiters of the human mind, of which they are in fact only the servants. Religion has provided a conception of life, and science travels in the beaten path. Religion reveals the meaning of life, and science only applies this meaning to the course of circumstances. And so, if religion falsifies the meaning of human life, science, which builds upon the same foundation, can only make manifest the same fantastic ideas.

According to the doctrine of the Church, men have a right to happiness, and this happiness is not the result of their own efforts, but of external causes. This conception has become the base of science and philosophy. Religion, science, and public opinion all unite in telling us that the life we now live is bad, and at the same time they affirm that the doctrine which teaches us how we can succeed in ameliorating life by becoming better, is an impracticable doctrine. Religion says that the doctrine of Jesus, which provides a reasonable method for the improvement of life by our own efforts, is impracticable because Adam fell and the world was plunged into sin. Philosophy says that the doctrine of Jesus is impracticable because human life is developed according to laws that are independent of the human will. In other words, the conclusions of science and philosophy are exactly the same as the conclusion reached by religion in the dogmas of original sin and the redemption.

There are two leading theses at the basis of the doctrine of the redemption: (1) the normal life of man is a life of happiness, but our life on earth is one of misery, and it can never be bettered by our own efforts; (2) our salvation is in faith, which enables us to escape from this life of misery. These two theses are the source of the religious conceptions of the believers and sceptics who make up our pseudo-Christian societies. The second thesis gave birth to the Church and its organization; from the first is derived the received tenets of public opinion and our political and philosophical theories. The germ of all political and philosophical theories that seek to justify the existing order of things such as Hegelianism and its offshoots is in this primal thesis. Pessimism, which demands of life what it cannot give and then denies its value, has also its origin in the same dogmatic proposition. Materialism, with its strange and enthusiastic affirmation that man is the product of natural forces and nothing more, is the legitimate result of the doctrine that teaches that life on earth is a degraded existence. Spiritism, with its learned adherents, is the best proof we have that the conclusions of philosophy and science are based upon the religious doctrine of that eternal happiness which should be the natural heritage of man.

This false conception of life has had a deplorable influence upon all reasonable human activity. The dogma of the fall and the redemption has debarred man from the most important and legitimate field for the exercise of his powers, and has deprived him entirely of the idea that he can of himself do any thing to make his life happier or better. Science and philosophy, proudly believing themselves hostile to pseudo-Christianity, only carry out its decrees. Science and philosophy concern themselves with everything except the theory that man can do any thing to make himself better or happier. Ethical and moral instruction have disappeared from our pseudo-Christian society without leaving a trace.

Believers and sceptics who concern themselves so little with the problem how to live, how to make use of the reason with which we are endowed, ask why our earthly life is not what they imagine it ought to be, and when it will become what they wish. This singular phenomenon is due to the false doctrine which has penetrated into the very marrow of humanity. The effects of the knowledge of good and evil, which man so unhappily acquired in paradise, do not seem to have been very lasting; for, neglecting the truth that life is only a solution of the contradictions between animal instincts and reason, he stolidly refrains from applying his reason to the discovery of the historical laws that govern his animal nature.

Excepting the philosophical doctrines of the pseudo-Christian world, all the philosophical and religious doctrines of which we have knowledge – Judaism, the doctrine of Confucius, Buddhism, Brahmanism, the wisdom of the Greeks – all aim to regulate human life, and to enlighten men with regard to what they must do to improve their condition. The doctrine of Confucius teaches the perfecting of the individual; Judaism, personal fidelity to an alliance with God; Buddhism, how to escape from a life governed by animal instincts; Socrates taught the perfecting of the individual through reason; the Stoics "recognized the independence of reason as the sole basis of the true life."

The reasonable activity of man has always been it could not be otherwise to light by the torch of reason his progress toward beatitude. Philosophy tells us that free will is an illusion, and then boasts of the boldness of such a declaration. Free will is not only an illusion; it is an empty word invented by theologians and experts in criminal law; to refute it would be to undertake a battle with a windmill. But reason, which illuminates our life and impels us to modify our actions, is not ail illusion, and its authority can never be denied. To obey reason in the pursuit of good is the substance of the teachings of all the masters of humanity, and it is the substance of the doctrine of Jesus; it is reason itself, and we cannot deny reason by the use of reason.

Making use of the phrase "son of man," Jesus teaches that all men have a common impulse toward good and toward reason, which leads to good. It is superfluous to attempt to prove that "Son of man" means "Son of God." To understand by the words "son of man" anything different from what they signify is to assume that Jesus, to say what he wished to say, intentionally made use of words which have an entirely different meaning. But even if, as the Church says, "son of man" means "Son of God," the phrase "son of man" applies none the less to man, for Jesus himself called all men "the Sons of God."

"The doctrine of the "son of man" finds its most complete expression in the interview with Nicodemus. Every man, Jesus says, aside from his consciousness of his material, individual life and of his birth in the flesh, has also a consciousness of a spiritual birth (John iii. 5, 6, 7), of an inner liberty, of something within; this comes from on high, from the infinite that we call God (John iii. 14–17); now it is this inner consciousness born of God, the son of God in man, that we must possess and nourish if we would possess true life. The son of man is homogeneous (of the same race) with God.

Whoever lifts up within himself this Son of God, whoever identifies his life with the spiritual life, will not deviate from the true way. Men wander from the way because they do not believe in this light which is within them, the light of which John speaks when he says, "In him was life; and the life teas the light of men." Jesus tells us to lift up the son of man, who is the Son of God, for a light to all men. When we have lifted up the son of man, we shall then know that we can do nothing without his guidance (John viii. 28). Asked, "Who is this son of man?" Jesus answers:

"Yet a little while is the light in you. Walk while ye have the light, lest darkness come upon you: for he that walketh in darkness knoweth not whither he goeth." (John xii. 35.)

The son of man is the light in every man that ought to illuminate his life. "Take heed therefore, that the light which is in thee be not darkness," is Jesus warning to the multitude (Luke xi. 30).

In all the different ages of humanity we find the same thought, that man is the receptacle of the divine light descended from heaven, and that this light is reason, which alone should be the object of our worship, since it alone can show the way to true well-being. This has been said by the Brahmins, by the Hebrew prophets, by Confucius, by Socrates, by Marcus Aurelius, by Epictetus, and by all the true sages, not by compilers of philosophical theories, but by men who sought goodness for them selves and for others. And yet we declare, in accordance with the dogma of the redemption that it is entirely superfluous to think of the light that is in us, and that we ought not to speak of it at all!

We must, say the believers, study the three persons of the Trinity; we must know the nature of each of these persons, and what sacraments we ought or ought not to perform, for our salvation depends, not on our own efforts, but on the Trinity and the regular performance of the sacraments. We must, say the sceptics, know the laws by which this infinitesimal particle of matter was evolved in infinite space and infinite time; but it is absurd to believe that by reason alone we can secure true well-being, because the amelioration of man's condition does not depend upon man himself, but upon the laws that we are trying to discover.

I firmly believe that, a few centuries hence, the history of what we call the scientific activity of this age will be a prolific subject for the hilarity and pity of future generations. For a number of centuries, they will say, the scholars of the western portion of a great continent were the victims of epidemic insanity; they imagined themselves to be the possessors of a life of eternal beatitude, and they busied themselves with divers lucubrations in which they sought to determine in what way this life could be realized, without doing any tiling themselves, or even concerning themselves with what they ought to do to Ameliorate the life which they already had. And what to the future historian will seem much more melancholy, it will be found that this group of men had once had a master who had taught them a number of simple and clear rules, pointing out what they must do to render their lives happy, and that the words of this master had been construed by some to mean that he would come on a cloud to reorganize human society, and by others as admirable doctrine, but impractical, since human life was not what they conceived it to be, and consequently was not worthy of consideration; as to human reason, it must concern itself with the study of the laws of an imaginary existence, without concerning itself about the welfare of the individual man.

The Church says that the doctrine of Jesus cannot be literally practised here on earth, because this earthly life is naturally evil, since it is only a shadow of the true life. The best way of living is to scorn this earthly existence, to be guided by faith (that is, by imagination) in a happy and eternal life to come, and to continue to live a bad life here and to pray to the good God.

Philosophy, science, and public opinion all say that the doctrine of Jesus is not applicable to human life as it now is, because the life of man does not depend upon the light of reason, but upon general laws; hence it is useless to try to live absolutely conformable to reason; we must live as we can with the firm conviction that according to the laws of historical and sociological progress, after having lived very imperfectly for a very long time, we shall suddenly find that our lives have become very good.

People come to a farm; they find there all that is necessary to sustain life, a house well furnished, barns filled with grain, cellars and storerooms well stocked with provisions, implements of husbandry, horses and cattle, in a word, all that is needed for a life of comfort and ease. Each wishes to profit by this abundance, but each for himself, without thinking of others, or of those who may come after him. Each wants the whole for himself, and begins to seize upon all that he can possibly grasp. Then begins a veritable pillage; they fight for the possession of the spoils; oxen and sheep are slaughtered; wagons and other implements are broken up into firewood; they fight for the milk and grain; they grasp more than they can consume. No one is able to sit down to the tranquil enjoyment of what he has, lest another take away the spoils already secured, to surrender them in turn to come on stronger. All these people leave the farm, bruised and famished. Thereupon the Master puts everything to rights, and arranges matters so that one may live there in peace. The farm is again a treasury of abundance. Then comes another group of seekers, and the same struggle and tumult is repeated, till these in their turn go away bruised and angry, cursing the Master for providing so little and so ill. The good Master is not discouraged; ho again provides for all that is needed to sustain life, and the same incidents are repeated over and over again.

Finally, among those who come to the farm, is one who says to his companions: "Comrades, how foolish we are; see how abundantly everything is supplied, how well everything is arranged! There is enough here for us and for those who will come after us; let us act in a reasonable manner. Instead of robbing each other, let us help one another. Let us work, plant, and care for the dumb animals, and every one will be satisfied." Some of the company understand what this wise person says; they cease from fighting and from robbing one another, and begin to work. But others, who have not heard the words of the wise man, or who distrust him, continue their former pillage of the Master's goods. This condition of things lasts for a long time. Those who have followed the counsels of the wise man say to those about them: "Cease from fighting, cease from wasting the Master's goods; you he better off for doing so; follow the wise man's advice." Nevertheless, a great many do not hear and will not believe, and matters go on very much as they did before.

All this is natural, and will continue as long as people do not believe the wise man's words. But, we are told, a time will come when every one on the farm will listen to and understand the words of the wise man, and will realize that God spoke through his lips, and that the wise man was himself none other than God in person; and all will have faith in his words. Meanwhile, instead of living according to the advice of the wise man, each struggles for his own, and they slay each other without pity, saying, "The struggle for existence is inevitable; we cannot do otherwise."

What does it all mean? Even the beasts graze in the fields without interfering with each other's needs, and men, after having learned the conditions of the true life, and after being convinced that God him self has shown them how to live the true life, follow still their evil ways, saying that it is impossible to live otherwise. What should we think of the people at the farm if, after having heard the words of the wise man, they had continued to live as before, snatching the bread from each other's mouths, fighting, and trying to grasp everything, to their own loss? We should say that they had misunderstood the wise man's words, and imagined things to be different from what they really were. The wise man said to them, "Your life here is bad; amend your ways, and it will become good." And they imagined that the wise man had condemned their life on the farm, and had promised them another and a better life somewhere else. They decided that the farm was only a temporary dwelling place, and that it was not worthwhile to try to live well there; the important thing was not to be cheated out of the other life promised them elsewhere. This is the only way in which we can explain the strange con duct of the people on the farm, of whom some believed that the wise man was God, and others that he was a man of wisdom, but all continued to live as before in defiance of the wise man's words. They understood everything but the one significant truth iii the wise man's teachings, that they must work out for themselves their own peace and happiness there on the farm, which they took for a temporary abode thinking all the time of the better life they were to possess elsewhere.

Here is the origin of the strange declaration that the precepts of the wise man were admirable, even divine, but that they were difficult to practise.

Oh, if men would only cease from evil ways while waiting for the Christ to come in his chariot of fire to their aid; if they would only cease to invoke the law of the differentiation or integration of forces, or any historical law whatever! None will come to their aid if they do not aid themselves. And to aid ourselves to a better life, we need expect nothing from heaven or from earth; we need only to cease from ways that result in our own loss.

Chapter 8

IF IT BE ADMITTED that the doctrine of Jesus is perfectly reasonable, and that it alone can give to men true happiness, what would be the condition of a single follower of that doctrine in the midst of a world that did not practise it at all? If all men would decide at the same time to obey, its practice would then be possible. But one man alone cannot act in defiance of the whole world; and so we hear continually this plea: "If, among men who do not practise the doctrine of Jesus, I alone obey it; if I give away all that I possess; if I turn the other cheek; if I refuse to take an oath or to go to war, I should find myself in profound isolation; if I did not die of hunger, I should be beaten; if I survived that, I should be cast into prison; I should be shot, and all the happiness of my life my life itself would be sacrificed in vain."

This plea is founded upon the doctrine of quid pro quo, which is the basis of all arguments against the possibility of practising the doctrine of Jesus. It is the current objection, and I sympathized with it in common with all the rest of the world, until I finally broke entirely away from the dogmas of the Church which prevented me from understanding the true significance of the doctrine of Jesus. Jesus proposed his doctrine as a means of salvation from the life of perdition organized by men contrary to his precepts; and I declared that 1 should be very glad to follow this doctrine if it were not for fear of this very perdition. Jesus offered me the true remedy against a life of perdition, and I clung to the belief of perdition from which it was plain that I did not consider this life as a life of perdition, but as something good, something real. The conviction that my personal, worldly life was something real and good constituted the misunderstanding, the obstacle, that prevented me from comprehending Jesus doctrine. Jesus knew the disposition of men to regard their personal, worldly life as real and good, and so, in a series of apothegms and parables, he taught them that they had no right to life, and that they were given life only that they might assure themselves of the true life by renouncing their worldly and fantastic organization of existence.

To understand what is meant by "saving" one's life, according to the doctrine of Jesus, we must first understand what the prophets, what Solomon, what Buddha, what all the wise men of the world have said about the personal life of man. But, as Pascal says, we cannot endure to think upon this theme, and so we carry always before us a screen to conceal the abyss of death, toward which we are constantly moving. It suffices to reflect on the isolation of the personal life of man, to be convinced that this life, in so far as it is personal, is not only of no account to each separately, but that it is a cruel jest to heart and reason. To understand the doctrine of Jesus, we must, before all, return to ourselves, reflect soberly, undergo the μετανοια of which John the Baptist, the precursor of Jesus, speaks, when addressing himself to men of clouded judgment. "Repent" (such was his preaching); "repent, have another mind, or you shall all perish. The axe is laid unto the root of the trees. Death and perdition await each one of you. Be warned, turn back, repent." And Jesus declared, "Except ye repent, ye shall all likewise perish." When Jesus was told of the death of the Galileans massacred by Pilate, he said:

"Suppose ye that these Galileans were sinners above all the Galileans, because they suffered such things? I tell you, Nay: but, except ye repent, ye shall all like wise perish. Or those eighteen upon whom the tower in Siloam fell, and slew them, think ye that they were sinners above all men that dwelt in Jerusalem? I tell you, Nay: but, except ye repent, ye shall all likewise perish." (Luke xiii. 1–5.)

If he had lived in our day, in Russia, he would have said: "Think you that those who perished in the circus at Berditchef or on the slopes of Koukouyef were sinners above all others? I tell you, No; but you, if you do not repent, if you do not arouse your selves, if you do not find in your life that which is imperishable, you also shall perish. You are horrified by the death of those crushed by the tower, burned in the circus; but your death, equally as frightful and as inevitable, is here, before you. You are wrong to conceal it or to forget it; unlocked for, it is only more hideous."

To the people of his own time he said: "When ye see a cloud rise out of the west, straight way ye say, There cometh a shower; and so it is. And when ye see the south wind blow, ye say, there will be heat; and it cometh to pass. Ye hypocrites, ye can discern the face of the sky and of the earth; but how is it that ye do not discern this time? Yea, and why even of yourselves judge ye not what is right?" (Luke xii. 54–57.)

We know how to interpret the signs of the weather; why, then, do we not see what is before us? It is in vain that we fly from danger, and guard our material life by all imaginable means; in spite of all, death is before us, if not in one way, then in another; if not by massacre, or the falling of a tower, then in our beds, amidst much greater suffering.

Make a simple calculation, as those do who undertake any worldly project, any enterprise whatever, such as the construction of a house, or the purchase of an estate, such as those make who labor with the hope of seeing their calculations realized.

"For which of you intending to build a tower, sitteth not down first, and counteth the cost whether he have sufficient to finish it? Lest haply, after he hath laid the foundation, and is not able to finish it, all that behold it begin to mock him, saying, This man began to build, and was not able to finish. Or what king, going to make war against another king, sitteth not down first and consulteth whether he be able with ten thousand to meet him that cometh against him with twenty thousand?" (Luke xiv. 28–31.)

Is it not the act of a madman to labor at what, under any circumstances, one can never finish? Death will always come before the edifice of worldly prosperity can be completed. And if we knew before hand that, however we may struggle with death, it is not we, but death, that will triumph; is it not an indication that we ought not to struggle with death, or to set our hearts upon that which will surely perish, but to seek to perform the task whose results cannot be destroyed by our inevitable departure?

"And he said unto his disciples, Therefore I say unto you, Take no thought for your life what ye shall eat; neither for the body, what ye shall put on. The life is more than meat and the body is more than raiment. Consider the ravens: for they neither sow nor reap; which neither have storehouse nor barn; and God feedeth them: How much more are ye better than the fowls? And which of you with taking thought can add to his stature one cubit? If ye then be not able to do that thing which is least, why take ye

thought for the rest? Consider the lilies how they grow: they toil not, they spin not; and yet I say unto you that Solomon in all his glory was not arrayed like one of these." (Luke xii. 22–27.)

Whatever pains we may take for our nourishment, for the care of the body, we cannot prolong life by a single hour. Is it not folly to trouble ourselves about a thing that we cannot possibly accomplish?

We know perfectly well that our material life will end with death, and we give ourselves up to evil to procure riches. Life cannot be measured by what we possess; if we think so, we only delude ourselves. Jesus tells us that the meaning of life does not lie in what we possess or in what we can accumulate, but in something entirely different. He says:

"The ground of a certain rich man brought forth plentifully: And he thought within himself, saying, What shall I do, because I have no room where to bestow my fruits? And he said, this will I do: I will pull down my barns, and build greater; and there will I bestow all my fruits and my goods. And I will say to my soul, soul, thou hast much goods laid up for many years; take thine ease, eat, drink, and be merry. But God said unto him, Thou fool, this night thy soul shall be required of thee: then whose shall those things be, which thou hast provided? So is he that layeth up treasure for himself, and is not rich toward God." (Luke xii. 15–21.)

Death threatens us every moment; Jesus says:

"Let your loins be girded about, and your lights burning; and ye yourselves like unto men that wait for their lord, when he will return from the wedding; that, when he cometh and knocketh, they may open unto him immediately. Blessed are those servants, whom the lord when he cometh shall find watching . . . . And if he shall come in the second watch, or come in the third watch, and find them so, blessed are those servants. And this know, that if the good man of the house had known what hour the thief would come, he would have watched, and not have suffered his house to be broken through. Be ye therefore ready also: for the son of man cometh at an hour when ye think not." (Luke xii. 35–40.)

The parable of the virgins waiting for the bride groom, that of the consummation of the age and the last judgment, as the commentators all agree, are designed to teach that death awaits us at every moment. Death awaits us at every moment. Life is passed in sight of death. If we labor for our selves alone, for our personal future, we know that what awaits us in the future is death. And death will destroy all the fruits of our labor. Consequently, a life for self can have no meaning. The reasonable life is different; it has another aim than the poor desires of a single individual. The reasonable life consists in living in such a way that life cannot be destroyed by death. We are troubled about many things, but only one thing is necessary.

From the moment of his birth, man is menaced by an inevitable peril, that is, by a life deprived of meaning, and a wretched death, if he does not discover the thing essential to the true life. Now it is precisely this one thing which insures the true life that Jesus reveals to men. He invents nothing, he promises nothing through divine power; side by side with this personal life, which is a delusion, he simply reveals to men the truth.

In the parable of the husbandmen (Matt. xxi. 33–42), Jesus explains the cause of that blindness in men which conceals the truth from them, and which impels them to take the apparent for the real, their personal life for the true life. Certain men, having leased a vineyard, imagined that they were its masters. And this delusion leads them into as cries of foolish and cruel actions, which ends in their exile. So each one of us imagines that life is his personal property, and that he has a right to enjoy it in such a way as may seem to him good, without recognizing any obligation to others. And the inevitable consequence of this delusion is a series of foolish and cruel actions followed by exclusion from life. And as the husbandmen killed the servants and at last the son of the householder, thinking that the more cruel they were, the better able they would be to gain their ends, so we imagine that we shall obtain the greatest security by means of violence.

Expulsion, the inevitable sentence visited upon the husbandmen for having taken to themselves the fruits of the vineyard, awaits also all men who imagine that the personal life is the true life. Death expels them from life; they are replaced by others, as a consequence of the error which led them to misconceive the meaning of life. As the husband men forgot, or did not wish to remember, that they had received a vineyard already hedged about and provided with winepress and tower, that someone had labored for them and expected them to labor in their turn for others; so the men who would live for themselves forget, or do not wish to remember, all that has been done for them during their life; they forget that they are under an obligation to labor in their turn, and that all the blessings of life which they enjoy are fruits that they ought to divide with others.

This new manner of looking at life, this μετανοια, or repentance, is the cornerstone of the doctrine of Jesus. According to this doctrine, men ought to understand and feel that they are insolvent, as the husbandmen should have understood and felt that they were insolvent to the householder, unable to pay the debt contracted by generations past, present, and to come, with the overruling power. They ought to feel that every hour of their existence is for the redemption of this debt, and that every man who, by a selfish life, rejects this obligation, separates himself from the principle of life, and so forfeits life. Each one should remember that in striving to save his own life, his personal life, he loses the true life, as Jesus so many times said. The true life is the life which adds something to the store of happiness accumulated by past generations, which increases this heritage in the present, and hands it down to the future. To take part in this true life, man should renounce his personal will for the will of the Father, who gives this life to man. In John viii. 35, we read:

"And the servant abideth not in the house forever: but the son abideth forever."

That is, only the son who observes the will of the father shall have eternal life. Now, the will of the Father of Life is not the personal, selfish life, but the life of the son of man; and so a man saves his life when he considers it as a pledge, as something confided to him by the Father for the profit of all, as something with which to live the life of the son of man.

A man, about to travel into a far country, called his servants together and divided among them his goods. Although receiving no precise instructions as to the manner in which they were to use these goods, some of the servants understood that the goods still belonged to the master, and that they ought to employ them for the master's gain. And the servants who had labored for the good of the master were rewarded, while the others, who had not so labored, were despoiled even of what they had received. (Matt. xxv. 14–46.)

The life of the son of man has been given to all men, and they know not why. Some of them under stand that life is not for their personal use, but that they must use it for the good of the son of man; others, feigning not to understand the true object of life, refuse to labor for the son of man; and those that labor for the true life will be united with the source of life; those that do not so labor, will lose the life they already have. Jesus tells us in what the service of the son of man consists and what will be the recompense of that service. The son of man, endowed with kingly authority, will call upon the faithful to inherit the true life; they have fed the hungry, given drink to the thirsty, clothed and con soled the wretched, and in so doing they have ministered to the son of man, who is the same in all men; they have not lived the personal life, but the life of the son of man, and they are given the life eternal.

According to all the Gospels, the object of Jesus teaching was the life eternal. And, strange as it may seem, Jesus, who is supposed to have been raised in person, and to have promised a general resurrection, Jesus not only said nothing in affirmation of individual resurrection and individual immortality beyond the grave, but on the contrary, every time that he met with this superstition (introduced at this period into the Talmud, and of which there is not a trace in the records of the Hebrew prophets), he did not fail to deny its truth. The Pharisees and the Sadducees were constantly discussing the subject of the resurrection of the dead. The Pharisees believed in the resurrection of the dead, in angels, and in spirits (Acts xxiii. 8), but the Sadducees did not believe in resurrection, or angel, or spirit. We do not know the source of the difference in belief, but it is certain that it was one of the polemical subjects among the secondary questions of the Hebraic doctrine that were constantly under discussion in the synagogues. And Jesus not only did not recognize the resurrection, but denied it every time he met with the idea. When the Sadducees demanded of Jesus, supposing that he believed with the Pharisees in the resurrection, to which of the seven brethren the woman should belong, he refuted with clearness and precision the idea of individual resurrection, saying that on this subject they erred, knowing neither the Scriptures nor the power of God. Those who are worthy of resurrection, he said, will remain like the angels of heaven (Mark xii. 21–24); and with regard to the dead:

"Have ye not read in the book of Moses, how in the bush God spake unto him, saying, I am the God of Abraham, and the God of Isaac, and the God of Jacob? He is not the God of the dead, but the God of the living: ye, therefore, do greatly err." (Mark xii. 26, 27.)

Jesus' meaning was that the dead are living in God. God said to Moses, "I am the God of Abraham, and of Isaac, and of Jacob." To God, all those who have lived the life of the son of man, are living. Jesus affirmed only this that, whoever lives in God, will be united to God; and he admitted no other idea of the resurrection. As to personal resurrection, strange as it may appear to those who have never carefully studied the Gospels for themselves, Jesus said nothing about it whatever.

If, as the theologians teach, the foundation of the Christian faith is the resurrection of Jesus, is it not strange that Jesus, knowing of his own resurrection, knowing that in this consisted the principal dogma of faith in him is it not strange that Jesus did not speak of the matter at least once, in clear and precise terms? Now, according to the canonical Gospels, he not only did not speak of it in clear and precise terms; he did not speak of it at all, not once, not a single word.

The doctrine of Jesus consisted in the elevation of the son of man, that is, in the recognition on the part of man, that he, man, was the Son of God. In his own individuality Jesus personified the man who has recognized the filial relation with God. He asked his disciples whom men said that he was the son of man? His disciples replied that some took him for John the Baptist, and some for Elijah. Then came the question, "But whom say ye that I am?" And Peter answered, "Thou art the Messiah, the son of the living God." Jesus responded, "Flesh and blood hath not revealed it unto thee, but my Father which is in heaven;" meaning that Peter understood, not through faith in human explanations, but because, feeling himself to be the son of God, he understood that Jesus was also the son of God. And after having explained to Peter that the true faith is founded upon the perception of the filial relation to God, Jesus charged his other disciples that they should tell no man that he was the Messiah. After this, Jesus told them that although he might suffer many things and be put to death, he, that is his doctrine, would be triumphantly re-established. And these words are interpreted as a prophecy of the resurrection (Matt. xvi. 13–21).

Of the thirteen passages 1 which are interpreted as prophecies of Jesus in regard to his own resurrection, two refer to Jonah in the whale's belly, another to the rebuilding of the temple. The others affirm that the son of man shall not be destroyed; but there is not a word about the resurrection of Jesus. In none of these passages is the word "resurrection" found in the original text. Ask anyone who is ignorant of theological interpretations, but who knows Greek, to translate them, and he will never agree with the received versions. In the original we find two different words, ανιϛτημι and εγειρω, which are rendered in the sense of resurrection; one of these words means to "re-establish;" the other means "to awaken, to rise up, to arouse one's self." But neither the one nor the other can ever, in any case, mean to "resuscitate" to raise from the dead. With regard to these Greek words and the corresponding Hebrew word, *qum*, we have only to examine the scriptural passages where these words are employed, as they are very frequently, to see that in no case is the meaning "to resuscitate" admissible. The word *voskresnovit, aitferstehn, resusciter* "to resuscitate" did not exist in the Greek or Hebrew tongues, for the reason that the conception corresponding to this word did not exist. To express the idea of resurrection in Greek or in Hebrew, it is necessary to employ a periphrasis, meaning, "is arisen, has awakened among the dead." Thus, in the Gospel of Matthew (xiv. 2) where reference is made to Herod's belief that John the Baptist had been resuscitated, we read, αυτός ηγέρθη από των νεκρών "has awakened among the dead." In the same manner, in Luke (xvi. 31), at the close of the parable of Lazarus, where it said that if men believe not the prophets, they would not believe even though one be resuscitated, we find the periphrasis, εαν τις εκ νεκρών αναστή "if one arose among the dead." But, if in these passages the words "among the dead" were not added to the words "arose or awakened," the last two could never signify resuscitation. When Jesus spoke of himself, he did not once use the words "among the dead" in any of the passages quoted in support of the affirmation that Jesus foretold his own resurrection.

Our conception of the resurrection is so entirely foreign to any idea that the Hebrews possessed with regard to life, that we cannot even imagine how Jesus would have been able to talk to them of the resurrection, and of an eternal, individual life, which should be the lot of every man. The idea of a future eternal life comes neither from Jewish doctrine nor from the doctrine of Jesus, but from an entirely different source. We are obliged to believe that belief in a future life is a primitive and crude conception based upon a confused idea of the resemblance between death and sleep, an idea common to all savage races.

The Hebraic doctrine (and much more the Christian doctrine) was far above this conception. But we are so convinced of the elevated character of this superstition, that we use it as a proof of the superiority of our doctrine to that of the Chinese or the Hindus, who do not believe in it at all. Not the theologians only, but the freethinkers, the learned historians of religions, such as Tiele, and Max Miller, make use of the same argument. In their classification of religions, they give the first place to those which recognize the superstition of the resurrection, and declare them to be far superior to those not professing that belief. Schopenhauer boldly denounced the Hebraic religion as the most despicable of all religions because it contains not a trace of this belief. Not only the idea itself, but all means of expressing it, were wanting to the Hebraic religion. Eternal life is in Hebrew *chayai oïlom*. By *oïlom* is meant the infinite, that which is permanent in the limits of time; *oïlom* also means "world" or "cosmos." Universal life, and much more *chayai oïlom*, "eternal life," is, according to the Jewish doctrine, the attribute of God alone. God is the God of life, the living God. Man, according to the Hebraic idea, is always mortal. God alone is always living. In the Pentateuch, the expression "eternal life" is twice met with; once in Deuteronomy and once in Genesis. God is represented as saying:

"See now that I, even I, am he, And there is no god with me: I

kill, and I make alive; I have wounded, and I heal: And there is
none that can deliver out of my hand.
For I lift up my hand to heaven, and say, As I live forever."
(Deut. xxxii. 39, 40.)

"*And Jehovah said, Behold, the man is become as one of us, to*
know good and evil; and now, lest he put forth his hand, and take
also the tree of life, and live forever." (Gen. iii. 22.)

These two sole instances of the use of the expression "eternal life" in the Old Testament (with the exception of another instance in the apocryphal book of Daniel) determine clearly the
Hebraic conception of the life of man and the life eternal. Life
itself, according to the Hebrews, is eternal, is in God; but man
is always mortal: it is his nature to be so. According to the Jewish doctrine, man as man, is mortal. He has life only as it passes
from one generation to another, and is so perpetuated in a race.
According to the Jewish doctrine, the faculty of life exists in the
people. When God said, "Ye may live, and not die," he addressed
these words to the people. The life that God breathed into man
is mortal for each separate human being; this life is perpetuated
from generation to generation, if men fulfil the union with God,
that is, obey the conditions imposed by God. After having propounded the Law, and having told them that this Law was to be
found not in heaven, but in their own hearts, Moses said to the
people:

"*See, I have set before thee this day life and good, and death*
and evil; in that I command thee this day to love the Eternal, to
walk in his ways, and to keep his commandments, that thou may-
est live. I call heaven and earth to witness against you this day,
that I have set before thee life and death, the blessing and the
curse: therefore choose life, that thou mayest live, thou and thy
seed: to love the Eternal, to obey his voice, and to cleave unto him:
for he is thy life, and the length of thy days." (Deut. xxx. 15–19.)

The principal difference between our conception of human life
and that possessed by the Jews is, that while we believe that our
mortal life, transmitted from generation to generation, is not the
true life, but a fallen life, a life temporarily depraved, the Jews, on
the contrary, believed this life to be the true and supreme good,
given to man on condition that he obey the will of God. From

our point of view, the transmission of the fallen life from generation to generation is the transmission of a curse; from the Jewish point of view, it is the supreme good to which man can attain, on condition that he accomplish the will of God. It is precisely upon the Hebraic conception of life that Jesus founded his doctrine of the true or eternal life, which he contrasted with the personal and mortal life. Jesus said to the Jews:

"Search the Scriptures; for in them ye think ye have eternal life: and they are they which testify of me." (John v. 39.)

To the young man who asked what he must do to have eternal life, Jesus said in reply, *"If thou, wilt enter into life, keep the commandments."* He did not say "the eternal life," but simply "the life" (Matt. xix. 17). To the same question propounded by the scribe, the answer was, "This do, and thou shalt live" (Luke x. 28), once more promising life, but saying nothing of eternal life. From these two instances, we know what Jesus meant by eternal life; whenever he made use of the phrase in speaking to the Jews, he employed it in exactly the same sense in which it was expressed in their own law, the accomplishment of the will of God. In contrast with the life that is temporary, isolated, and personal, Jesus taught of the eternal life promised by God to Israel with this difference, that while the Jews believed the eternal life was to be perpetuated solely by their chosen people, and that whoever wished to possess this life must follow the exceptional laws given by God to Israel, the doctrine of Jesus holds that the eternal life is perpetuated in the son of man, and that to obtain it we must practise the commandments of Jesus, who summed up the will of God for all humanity.

As opposed to the personal life, Jesus taught us, not of a life beyond the grave, but of that universal life which comprises within itself the life of humanity, past, present, and to come. According to the Jewish doctrine, the personal life could be saved from death only by accomplishing the will of God as propounded in the Mosaic law. On this condition only the life of the Jewish race would not perish, but would pass from generation to generation of the chosen people of God. According to the doctrine of Jesus, the personal life is saved from death by the accomplishment of the will of God as propounded in the commandments of Jesus.

On this condition alone the personal life does not perish, but becomes eternal and immutable, in union with the son of man. The difference is, that while the religion given by Moses was that of a people for a national God, the religion of Jesus is the expression of the aspirations of all humanity. The perpetuity of life in the posterity of a people is doubtful, because the people itself may disappear, and perpetuity depends upon a posterity in the flesh. Perpetuity of life, according to the doctrine of Jesus, is indubitable, because life, according to his doctrine, is an attribute of all humanity in the son of man who lives in harmony with the will of God.

If we believe that Jesus words concerning the last judgment and the consummation of the age, and other words reported in the Gospel of John, are a promise of a life beyond the grave for the souls of men, if we believe this, it is none the less true that his teachings in regard to the light of life and the kingdom of God have the same meaning for us that they had for his hearers eighteen centuries ago; that is, that the only real life is the life of the son of man conformable to the will of the Giver of Life. It is easier to admit this than to admit that the doctrine of the true life, conformable to the will of the Giver of Life, contains the promise of the immortality of life beyond the grave.

Perhaps it is right to think that man, after this terrestrial life passed in the satisfaction of personal desires, will enter upon the possession of an eternal personal life in paradise, there to taste all imaginable enjoyments; but to believe that this is so, to endeavor to persuade ourselves that for our good actions we shall be recompensed with eternal felicity, and for our bad actions punished with eternal torments, to believe this, does not aid us in under standing the doctrine of Jesus, but, on the contrary, takes away the principal foundation of that doctrine. The entire doctrine of Jesus inculcates renunciation of the personal, imaginary life, and a merging of this personal life in the universal life of humanity, in the life of the son of man. Now the doctrine of the individual immortality of the soul does Does not impel us to renounce the personal life; on the contrary, it affirms the continuance of individuality forever.

The Jews, the Chinese, the Hindus, all men who do not believe in the dogma of the fall and the redemption, conceive of life as it is. A man lives, is united with a woman, engenders children, cares for them, grows old, and dies. His life continues in his children, and so passes on from one generation to another, like everything else in the world, stones, metals, earth, plants, animals, stars. Life is life, and we must make the best of it.

To live for self alone, for the animal life, is not reasonable. And so men, from their earliest existence, have sought for some reason for living aside from the gratification of their own desires; they live for their children, for their families, for their nation, for humanity, for all that does not die with the personal life.

But according to the doctrine of the Church, human life, the supreme good that we possess, is but a very small portion of another life of which we are deprived for a season. Our life is not the life that God intended to give us or such as is our due. Our life is degenerate and fallen, a mere fragment, a mockery, compared with the real life to which we think ourselves entitled. The principal object of life is not to try to live this mortal life conformably to the will of the Giver of Life; or to render it eternal in the generations, as the Hebrews believed; or to identify ourselves with the will of God, as Jesus taught; no, it is to believe that after this unreal life the true life will begin.

Jesus did not speak of the imaginary life that we believe to be our due, and that God did not give to us for some unexplained reason. The theory of the fall of Adam, of eternal life in paradise, of an immortal soul breathed by God into Adam, was unknown to Jesus; he never spoke of it, never made the slightest allusion to its existence. Jesus spoke of life as it is, as it must be for all men; we speak of an imaginary life that has never existed. How, then, can we understand the doctrine of Jesus?

Jesus did not anticipate such a singular change of view in his disciples. He supposed that all men understood that the destruction of the personal life is inevitable, and he revealed to them an imperishable life. He offers true peace to them that suffer; but to those who believe that they are certain to possess more than Jesus gives, his doctrine can be of no value. How shall I persuade a man to toil in return for food and clothing if this man is persuaded that he already possesses great riches? Evidently he will pay no attention to my exhortations. So it is with regard to the doctrine of Jesus. Why should I toil for bread when I can be rich without labor? Why should I trouble myself to live this life according to the will of God when I am sure of a personal life for all eternity?

That Jesus Christ, as the second person of the Trinity, as God made manifest in the flesh, was the salvation of men; that he took upon himself the penalty for the sin of Adam and the sins of all men; that he atoned to the first person of the Trinity for the sins of humanity; that he instituted the Church and the sacraments for our salvation believing this, the Church says, we are saved, and shall possess a personal, immortal life beyond the grave. But meanwhile we cannot deny that Jesus saved and still saves men by revealing to them their inevitable loss, showing them that he is the way, the truth, and the life, the true way to life instead of the false way to the personal life that men had heretofore followed.

If there are any who doubt the life beyond the grave and salvation based upon redemption, no one can doubt the salvation of all men, and of each individual man, if they will accept the evidence of the destruction of the personal life, and follow the true way to safety by bringing their personal wills into harmony with the will of God. Let each man endowed with reason ask himself, what is life? And what is death? And let him try to give to life and death any other meaning than that revealed by Jesus, and he will find that any attempt to find in life a meaning not based upon the renunciation of self, the service of humanity, of the son of man, is utterly futile. It cannot be doubted that the personal life is condemned to destruction, and that a life conformable to the will of God alone gives the possibility of salvation. It is not much in comparison with the sublime belief in the future life! It is not much, but it is sure.

I am lost with my companions in a snow storm. One of them assures me with the utmost sincerity that he sees a light in the distance, but it is only a mirage which deceives us both; we strive to reach this light, but we never can find it. Another resolutely brushes away the snow; he seeks and finds the road, and he cries to us, "Go not that way, the light you see is false, you will wander to destruction; here is the road, I feel it beneath my feet; we are saved." It is very little, we say. We had faith in that light that gleamed in our deluded eyes, that told us of a refuge, a warm shelter, rest, deliverance, and now in exchange for it we have nothing but the road. Ah, but if we continue to travel toward the imaginary light, we shall perish; if we follow the road, we shall surely arrive at a haven of safety.

What, then, must I do if I alone understand the doctrine of Jesus, and I alone have trust in it among a people who neither understand it nor obey it? What ought I to do to live like the rest of the world, or to live according to the doctrine of Jesus? I understood the doctrine of Jesus as expressed in his commandments, and I believed that the practice of these commandments would bring happiness to me and to all men. I understood that the fulfilment of these commandments is the will of God, the source of life. More than this, I saw that I should die like a brute after a farcical existence if I did not fulfil the will of God, and that the only chance of salvation lay in the fulfilment of His will. In following the example of the world about me, I should unquestionably act contrary to the welfare of all men, and, above all, contrary to the will of the Giver of Life; I should surely forfeit the sole possibility of bettering my desperate condition. In following the doctrine of Jesus, I should continue the work common to all men who had lived before me; I should contribute to the welfare of my fellows, and of those who were to live after me; I should obey the command of the Giver of Life; I should seize upon the only hope of salvation.

The circus at Berditchef is in flames. A crowd of people are struggling before the only place of exit, a door that opens inward. Suddenly, in the midst of the crowd, a voice rings out: "Back, stand back from the door; the closer you press against it, the less the chance of escape; stand back; that is your only chance of safety!" Whether I am alone in understanding this command, or whether others with me also hear and understand, I have but one duty, and that is, from the moment I have heard and understood, to fall back from the door and to call upon every one to obey the voice of the saviour. I may be suffocated, I may be crushed beneath the feet of the multitude, I may perish; my sole chance of safety is to do the one thing necessary to gain an exit. And I can do nothing else. A saviour should be a saviour, that is, one who saves. And the salvation of Jesus is the true salvation. He came, he preached his doctrine, and humanity is saved. The circus may burn in an hour, and those penned up in it may have no time to escape. But the world has been burning for eighteen hundred years; it has burned ever since Jesus said, *"I am come to send fire on the earth;"* and I suffer as it burns, and it will continue to burn until humanity is saved. Was not this fire kindled that men might have the felicity of salvation? Understanding this, I understood and believed that Jesus is not only the Messiah, that is, the Anointed One, the Christ, but that he is in truth the Saviour of the world. I know that he is the only way, that there is no other way for me or for those who are tormented with me in this life. I know, that for me as for all, there is no other safety than the fulfilment of the commandments of Jesus, who gave to all humanity the greatest conceivable sum of benefits.

Would there be great trials to endure? Should I die in following the doctrine of Jesus? This question did not alarm me. It might seem frightful to anyone who does not realize the nothingness and absurdity of an isolated personal life, and who believes that he will never die. But I know that my life, considered in relation to my individual happiness, is, taken by itself, a stupendous farce, and that this meaningless existence will end in a stupid death. Knowing this, I have nothing to fear. I shall die as others die who do not observe the doctrine of Jesus; but my life and my death will have a meaning for myself and for others. My life and my death will have added something to the life and salvation of others, and this will be in accordance with the doctrine of Jesus.

Chapter 9

L ET ALL THE WORLD PRACTISE the doctrine of Jesus, and the reign of God will come upon earth; if I alone practise it, I shall do what I can to better my own condition and the condition of those about me. There is no salvation aside from the fulfilment of the doctrine of Jesus. But who will give me the strength to practise it, to follow it without ceasing, and never to fail? "Lord, I believe; help thou mine unbelief." The disciples called upon Jesus to strengthen their faith. "When I would do good," says the apostle Paul, "evil is present with me." It is hard to work out one's salvation.

A drowning man calls for aid. A rope is thrown to him, and he says: "Strengthen my belief that this rope will save me. I believe that the rope will save me; but help my unbelief." What is the meaning of this? If a man will not seize upon his only means of safety, it is plain that he does not under stand his condition.

How can a Christian who professes to believe in the divinity of Jesus and of his doctrine, whatever may be the meaning that he attaches thereto, say that he wishes to believe, and that he cannot believe? God comes upon earth, and says, "Fire, torments, eternal darkness await you; and here is your salvation – fulfil my doctrine." It is not possible that a believing Christian should not believe and profit by the salvation thus offered to him; it is not possible that he should say, "Help my unbelief." If a man says this, he not only does not believe in his perdition, but he must be certain that he shall not perish.

A number of children have fallen from a boat into the water. For an instant their clothes and their feeble struggles keep them on the surface of the stream, and they do not realize their danger. Those in the boat throw out a rope. They warn the children against their peril, and urge them to grasp the rope (the parables of the woman and the piece of silver, the shepherd and the lost sheep, the marriage feast, the prodigal son, all have this meaning), but the children do not believe; they refuse to believe, not in the rope, but that they are in danger of drowning. Children as frivolous as themselves have assured them that they can continue to float gaily along even when the boat is far away. The children do not believe; but when their clothes are saturated, the strength of their little arms exhausted, they will sink and perish. This they do not believe, and so they do not believe in the rope of safety.

Just as the children in the water will not grasp the rope that is thrown to them, persuaded that they will not perish, so men who believe in the resurrection of the soul, convinced that there is no danger, do not practise the commandments of Jesus. They do not believe in what is certain, simply because they do believe in what is uncertain. It is for this cause they cry, "Lord, strengthen our faith, lest we perish." But this is impossible. To have the faith that will save them from perishing, they must cease to do what will lead them to perdition, and they must begin to do something for their own safety; they must grasp the rope of safety. Now this is exactly what they do not wish to do; they wish to persuade themselves that they will not perish, although they see their comrades perishing one after another before their very eyes. They wish to persuade themselves of the truth of what does not exist, and so they ask to be strengthened in faith. It is plain that they have not enough faith, and they wish for more.

When I understood the doctrine of Jesus, I saw that what these men call faith is the faith denounced by the apostle James:

"What doth it profit, my brethren, if a man believe he hath faith, but hath not works? Can that faith save him? If a brother or sister be naked and in lack of daily food, and one of you say unto them, Go in peace, be ye warmed and filled; and yet ye give them not the things needful to the body; what doth it profit? Even so faith, if it have not works, is dead in itself. But someone will say, Thou hast faith, and I have works: Shew me thy faith which is without works, and I, by my works, will show thee my faith. Thou believest there is one God; thou doest well: the demons also believe, and tremble. But wilt thou know, vain man, that faith without works is dead? Was not Abraham our father justified by works when he offered up Isaac his son upon the altar? Thou seest that faith wrought with his works, and by works teas faith made perfect. ... Ye see that by works a man is justified, and not only by faith.

For as the body without the spirit is dead, so faith is dead without works." (James ii. 14–26.)

James says that the indication of faith is the acts that it inspires, and consequently that a faith which does not result in acts is of words merely, with which one cannot feed the hungry, or justify belief, or obtain salvation. A faith without acts is not faith. It is only a disposition to believe in something, a vain affirmation of belief in something in which one does not really believe. Faith, as the apostle James defines it, is the motive power of actions, and actions are a manifestation of faith.

The Jews said to Jesus: What signs shewest thou then, that we may see, and believe thee? What dost thou work?" (John vi. 30. See also Mark xv. 32; Matt, xxvii. 42). Jesus told them that their desire was vain, and that they could not be made to believe what they did not believe. "If I tell you," he said, "ye will not believe" (Luke xxii. 67); "I told you, and ye believed not. . . . But ye believe not because ye are not of my sheep" (John x. 25, 26).

The Jews asked exactly what is asked by Christians brought up in the Church; they asked for some outward sign which should make them believe in the doctrine of Jesus. Jesus explained that this was impossible, and he told them why it was impossible. He told them that they could not believe because they were not of his sheep; that is, they did not follow the road he had pointed out. He explained why some believed, and why others did not believe, and he told them what faith really was. He said: "How can ye believe which receive your doctrine δοξα one of another, and seek not the doctrine that cometh only from God?" (John v.).

To believe, Jesus says, we must seek for the doctrine that comes from God alone.

"He that speaketh of himself seeketh (to extend) his own doctrine, δοξαν την ιδιαν but he that seeketh (to extend) the doctrine of him that sent him, the same is true, and no untruth is in him." (John vii. 18.)

The doctrine of life is the foundation of faith, and actions result spontaneously from faith. But there are two doctrines of life: Jesus denies the one and affirms the other. One of these doctrines, a source of all error, consists of the idea that the personal life is one of the essential and real attributes of man. This doctrine has been followed, and is still followed, by the majority of men; it is the source of divergent beliefs and acts. The other doctrine, taught by Jesus and by all the prophets, affirms that our personal life has no meaning save through fulfilment of the will of God. If a man confess a doctrine that emphasizes his own personal life, he will consider that his personal welfare is the most important thing in the world, and he will consider riches, honors, glory, pleasure, as true sources of happiness; he will have a faith in accordance with his inclination, and his acts will always be in harmony with his faith. If a man confess a different doctrine, if he find the essence of life in fulfilment of the will of God in accordance with the example of Abraham and the teaching and example of Jesus, his faith will accord with his principles, and his acts will be conformable to his faith. And so those who believe that true happiness is to be found in the personal life can never have faith in the doctrine of Jesus. All their efforts to fix their faith upon it will be always vain. To believe in the doctrine of Jesus, they must look at life in an entirely different way. Their actions will coincide always with their faith and not with their intentions and their words.

In men who demand of Jesus that lie shall work miracles we may recognize a desire to believe in his doctrine; but this desire never can be realized in life, however arduous the efforts to obtain it. In vain they pray, and observe the sacraments, and give in charity, and build churches, and convert others; they cannot follow the example of Jesus because their acts are inspired by a faith based upon an entirely different doctrine from that which they confess. They could not sacrifice an only son as Abraham was ready to do, although Abraham had no hesitation whatever as to what he should do, just as Jesus and his disciples were moved to give their lives for others, because such action alone constituted for them the true meaning of life. This incapacity to understand the substance of faith explains the strange moral state of men, who, acknowledging that they ought to live in accordance with the doctrine of Jesus, endeavor to live in opposition to this doctrine, conformably to their belief that the personal life is a sovereign good.

The basis of faith is the meaning that we derive from life, the meaning that determines whether we look upon life as important and good, or trivial and corrupt. Faith is the appreciation of good and of evil. Men with a faith based upon their own doctrines do not succeed at all in harmonizing this faith with the faith inspired by the doctrine of Jesus; and so it was with the early disciples. This misapprehension is frequently referred to in the Gospels in clear and decisive terms. Several times the disciples asked Jesus to strengthen their faith in his words (Matt. xx. 20–28; Mark x. 35–48). After the message, so terrible to every man who believes in the personal life and who seeks his happiness in the riches of this world, after the words, "How hardly shall they that have riches enter into the kingdom of God" and after words still more terrible for men who believe only in the personal life, "Sell whatsoever thou hast and give to the poor;" after these warning words Peter asked, "Behold, we have forsaken all and followed thee; what shall we have therefore?" Then James and John and, according to the Gospel of Matthew, their mother, asked him that they might be allowed to sit with him in glory. They asked Jesus to strengthen their faith with a promise of future recompense. To Peter's question Jesus replied with a parable (Matt. xx. 1–16); to James he replied that they did not know what they asked; that they asked what was impossible; that they did not understand the doctrine, which meant a renunciation of the personal life, while they demanded personal glory, a personal recompense; that they should drink the cup he drank of (that is, live as he lived), but to sit upon his right hand and upon his left was not his to give. And Jesus added that the great of this world had their profit and enjoyment of glory and personal power only in the worldly life; but that his disciples ought to know that the true meaning of human life is not in personal happiness, but in ministering to others; "the son of man came not to be ministered unto, but to minister, and to give his life a ransom for many." In reply to the unreasonable demands which revealed their slowness to understand his doctrine, Jesus did not command his disciples to have faith in his doctrine, that is, to modify the ideas inspired by their own doctrine (he knew that to be impossible), but he explained to them the meaning of that life which is the basis of true faith, that is, taught them how to discern good from evil?

To Peter's question, "What shall we receive?" Jesus replies with the parable of the laborers in the vineyard (Matt. xx. 1–16), beginning with the words "For the Kingdom of heaven is like unto a man that is a householder," and by this means Jesus explains to Peter that failure to understand the doctrine is the cause of lack of faith; and that remuneration in proportion to the amount of work done is important only from the point of view of the personal life.

This faith is based upon the presumption of certain imaginary rights; but a man has a right to nothing; he is under obligations for the good he has received, and so he can exact nothing. Even if he were to give up his whole life to the service of others, he could not pay the debt he has incurred, and so he cannot complain of injustice. If a man sets a value upon his rights to life, if he keeps a reckoning with the Overruling Power from whom he has received life, he proves simply that he does not understand the meaning of life. Men who have received a benefit act far otherwise. The laborers employed in the vineyard were found by the householder idle and unhappy; they did not possess life in the proper meaning of the term. And then the householder gave them the supreme welfare of life, work. They accepted the benefits offered, and were discontented because their remuneration was not graduated according to their imaginary deserts. They did the work, believing in their false doctrine of life and work as a right, and consequently with an idea of the remuneration to which they were entitled. They did not understand that work is the supreme good, and that they should be thankful for the opportunity to work, instead of exacting payment. And so all men who look upon life as these laborers looked upon it, never can possess true faith. This parable of the laborers, related by Jesus in response to the request by his disciples that he strengthen their faith, shows more clearly than ever the basis of the faith that Jesus taught.

When Jesus told his disciples that they must forgive a brother who trespassed against them not only once, but seventy times seven times, the disciples were overwhelmed at the difficulty of observing this injunction, and said, "Increase our faith" just as a little while before they had asked, "What shall we receive?" Now they uttered the language of would-be Christians: "We wish to believe, but cannot; strengthen our faith that we may be saved; make us believe" (as the Jews said to Jesus when they demanded miracles); "either by miracles or promises of recompense, make us to have faith in our salvation."

The disciples said what we all say: "How pleasant it would be if we could live our selfish life, and at the same time believe that it is far better to practise the doctrine of God by living for others." This disposition of mind is common to us all; it is contrary to the meaning of the doctrine of Jesus, and yet we are astonished at our lack of faith. Jesus disposed of this misapprehension by means of a parable illustrating true faith. Faith cannot come of confidence in his words; faith can come only of a consciousness of our condition; faith is based only upon the dictates of reason as to what is best to do in a given situation. He showed that this faith cannot be awakened in others by promises of recompense or threats of punishment, which can only arouse a feeble confidence that will fail at the first trial; but that the faith which removes mountains, the faith that nothing can shatter, is inspired by the consciousness of our inevitable loss if we do not profit by the salvation that is offered.

To have faith, we must not count on any promise of recompense; we must understand that the only way of escape from a ruined life is a life conform able to the will of the Master. He who understands this will not ask to be strengthened in his faith, but will work out his salvation without the need of any exhortation. The householder, when he comes from the fields with his workman, does not ask the latter to sit down at once to dinner, but directs him to attend first to other duties and to wait upon him, the master, and then to take his place at the table and dine. This the workman does without any sense of being wronged; he does not boast of his labor nor does he demand recognition or recompense, for he knows that labor is the inevitable condition of his existence and the true welfare of his life. So Jesus says that when we have done all that we are commanded to do, we have only fulfilled our duty. He who understands his relations to his master will understand that he has life only as he obeys the master's will; he will know in what his welfare consists, and he will have a faith that does not demand the impossible. This is the faith taught by Jesus, which has for its foundation a thorough perception of the true meaning of life. The source of faith is light:

"That was the true light which lighteth every man that cometh into the world. lie was in the world, and the world was made by him, and the world knew him not. He came unto his own, and his own received him not. But as many as received him, to them gave he the right to become the children of God, even to them that believe on his name." (John i. 9–12.)

"And this is the condemnation, that light is come into the world, and men loved darkness rather than light, because their deeds were evil. For everyone that doeth ill hateth the light, and cometh not to the light, lest his works should be reproved. But he that doeth the truth cometh to the light, that his works may be made manifest, because they have been wrought in God." (John iii. 19–21.)

He who understands the doctrine of Jesus will not ask to be strengthened in his faith. The doctrine of Jesus teaches that faith is inspired by the light of truth. Jesus never asked men to have faith in his person; he called upon them to have faith in truth. To the Jews he said:

"Ye seek to kill me, a man that hath told you the truth which I have heard of God." (John viii, 40.)

"Which of you convicteth me of sin? If I say truth, why do ye not believe me?" (John viii. 46.)

"To this end have I been born, and to this end am I come into the world, that I should bear witness unto the truth. Everyone that is of the truth heareth my voice." (John xviii. 37.)

To his disciples he said:

"I am the way, and the truth, and the life." (John xiv. 6.)

"The Father . . . shall give you another Comforter, that he may be with you forever, even the Spirit of truth: whom the world cannot receive; for it beholdeth him not, neither knoweth him: ye know him; for he abideth with you, and shall be in you." (John xiv. 16, 17.)

Jesus doctrine, then, is truth, and he himself is truth. The doctrine of Jesus is the doctrine of truth. Faith in Jesus is not belief in a system based upon his personality, but a consciousness of truth. No one can be persuaded to believe in the doctrine of Jesus, nor can anyone be stimulated by any promised reward to practise it. He who understands the doctrine of Jesus will have faith in him, because this doctrine is true. He who knows the truth indispensable to his happiness must believe in it, just as a man who knows that he is drowning grasps the rope of safety. Thus, the question, what must I do to believe? is an indication that he who asks it does not understand the doctrine of Jesus.

Chapter 10

WE SAY, IT IS DIFFICULT to live according to the doctrine of Jesus! And why should it not be difficult, when by our organization of life we carefully hide from ourselves our true situation; when we endeavor to persuade ourselves that our situation is not at all what it is, but that it is something else? We call this faith, and regarding it as sacred, we endeavor by all possible means, by threats, by flattery, by falsehood, by stimulating the emotions, to attract men to its support. In this mad determination to believe what is contrary to sense and reason, we reach such a degree of aberration that we are ready to take as an indication of truth the very absurdity of the object in whose behalf we solicit the confidence of men. Are there not Christians who are ready to declare with enthusiasm "*Credo quia absurdum,*" supposing that the absurd is the best medium for teaching men the truth? Not long ago a man of intelligence and great learning said to me that the Christian doctrine had no importance as a moral rule of life. Morality, he said, must be sought in the teachings of the Stoics and the Brahmins, and in the Talmud. The essence of the Christian doctrine is not in morality, he said, but in the theosophical doctrine propounded in its dogmas. According to this I ought to prize in the Christian doctrine not what it contains of eternal good to humanity, not its teachings indispensable to a reasonable life; I ought to regard as the most important element of Christianity that portion of it which it is impossible to understand, and therefore useless – and this in the name of the faith for which thousands of men have perished.

We have a false conception of life, a conception based upon wrong doing and inspired by selfish passions, and we consider our faith in this false conception (which we have in some way attached to the doctrine of Jesus), as the most important and necessary thing with which we are concerned. If men had not for centuries maintained faith in what is untrue, this false conception of life, as well as the truth of the doctrine of Jesus, would long ago have been revealed.

It is a terrible thing to say, but it seems to me that if the doctrine of Jesus, and that of the Church which has been foisted upon it, had never existed, those who today call themselves Christians would be much nearer than they are to the truth of the doctrine of Jesus; that is, to the reasonable doctrine which teaches the true meaning of life. The moral doctrines of all the prophets of the world would not then be closed to them. They would have their little ideas of truth, and would regard them with confidence. Now, all truth is revealed, and this truth has so horrified those whose manner of life it condemned, that they have disguised it in falsehood, and men have lost confidence in the truth.

In our European society, the words of Jesus, "To this end I am come into the world, that I shall bear witness unto the truth. Everyone that is of the truth heareth my voice" have been for a long time supplanted by Pilate's question, "What is truth?" This question, quoted as a bitter and profound irony against Roman, we have taken as of serious purport, and have made of it an article of faith.

With us, all men live not only without truth, not only without the least desire to know truth, but with the firm conviction that, among all useless occupations, the most useless is the endeavor to find the truth that governs human life. The rule of life, the doctrine that all peoples, excepting our European societies, have always considered as the most important thing, the rule of which Jesus spoke as the one thing needful, is an object of universal disdain. An institution called the Church, in which no one, not even if he belong to it, really believes, has for a long time usurped the place of this rule.

The only source of light for those who think and suffer is hidden. For a solution of the questions, what am I? What ought I to do? I am not allowed to depend upon the doctrine of him who came to save; I am told to obey the authorities, and believe in the Church. But why is life so full of evil? Why so much wrongdoing? May I not abstain from taking part therein? Is it impossible to lighten this heavy load that weighs me down? The reply is that this is impossible, that the desire to live well and to help others to live well is only a temptation of pride; that one thing is possible, to save one's soul for the future life. He who is not willing to take part in this miserable life may keep aloof from it; this way is open to all; but, says the doctrine of the Church, he who chooses this way can take no part in the life of the world; he ceases to live. Our masters tell us that there are only two ways, to believe in and obey the powers that be, to participate in the organized evil about us, or to forsake the world and take refuge in convent or monastery; to take part in the offices of the Church, doing nothing for men, and declaring the doctrine of Jesus impossible to practise, accepting the iniquity of life sanctioned by the Church, or to renounce life for what is equivalent to slow suicide.

However surprising the belief that the doctrine of Jesus is excellent, but impossible of practice, there is a still more surprising tradition that he who wishes to practise this doctrine, not in word, but in deed, must retire from the world. This erroneous belief that it is better for a man to retire from the world than to expose himself to temptations, existed amongst the Hebrews of old, but is entirely foreign, not only to the spirit of Christianity, but to that of the Jewish religion. The charming and significant story of the prophet Jonah, which Jesus so loved to quote, was written in regard to this very error. The prophet Jonah, wishing to remain upright and virtuous, retires from the perverse companionship of men.

But God shows him that as a prophet ho ought to communicate to misguided men a knowledge of the truth, and so ought not to fly from men, but ought rather to live in communion with them. Jonah, disgusted with the depravity of the inhabitants of Nineveh, flies from the city; but he cannot escape his vocation. He is brought back, and the will of God is accomplished; the Ninevites receive the words of Jonah and are saved. Instead of rejoicing that he has been made the instrument of God's will, Jonah is angry, and condemns God for the mercy shown the Ninevites, arrogating to himself alone the exercise of reason and goodness. He goes out into the desert and makes him a shelter, whence he addresses his reproaches to God. Then a gourd comes up over Jonah and protects him from the sun, but the next day it withers. Jonah, smitten by the heat, reproaches God anew for allowing the gourd to wither. Then God says to him:

"Thou hast had pity on the gourd, for the which thou hast not labored, neither madest it grow; which came up in a night, and perished in a night: and should I not have pity on Nineveh, that great city; wherein are more than six score thousand persons that cannot discern between their right hand and their left hand?"

Jesus knew this story, and often referred to it. In the Gospels we find it related how Jesus, after the interview with John, who had retired into the desert, was himself subjected to the same temptation before beginning his mission. He was led by the Spirit into the wilderness, and there tempted by the Devil (error), over which he triumphed and returned to Galilee. Thereafter he mingled with the most depraved men, and passed his life among publicans, Pharisees, and fishermen, teaching them the truth.

Even according to the doctrine of the Church, Jesus, as God in man, has given us the example of his life. All of his life that is known to us was passed in the company of publicans, of the downfallen, and of Pharisees. The principal commandments of Jesus are that his followers shall love others and spread his doctrine. Both exact constant communion with the world. And yet the deduction is made that the doctrine of Jesus permits retirement from the world. That is, to imitate Jesus we may do exactly contrary to what he taught and did himself.

As the Church explains it, the doctrine of Jesus offers itself to men of the world and to dwellers in monasteries, not as a rule of life for bettering one's own condition and the condition of others, but as a doctrine which teaches the man of the world how to live an evil life and at the same time gain for himself another life, and the monk how to render existence still more difficult than it naturally is. But Jesus did not teach this. Jesus taught the truth, and if metaphysical truth is the truth, it will remain such in practice. If life in God is the only true life, and is in itself profitable, then it is so here in this world in spite of all that may happen. If in this world a life in accordance with the doctrine of Jesus is not profitable, his doctrine cannot be true.

Jesus did not ask us to pass from better to worse, but, on the contrary, from worse to better. He had pity upon men, who to him were like sheep without a shepherd. He said that his disciples would be persecuted for his doctrine, and that they must bear the persecutions of the world with resolution. But he did not say that those who followed his doctrine would suffer more than those who followed the world's doctrine; on the contrary, he said that those who followed the world's doctrine would be wretched, and that those who followed his doctrine would have joy and peace. Jesus did not teach salvation by faith in asceticism or voluntary torture, but he taught us a way of life which, while saving us from the emptiness of the personal life, would give us less of suffering and more of joy. Jesus told men that in practising his doctrine among unbelievers they would be, not more unhappy, but, on the contrary, much more happy, than those who did not practise it. There was, he said, one infallible rule, and that was to have no care about the worldly life. When Peter said to Jesus, "We have forsaken all, and followed thee; what then shall we have?" Jesus replied:

"There is no man that hath left house, or brethren, or sisters, or mother, or father, or children, or lands, for my sake, and for the gospel's sake, but he shall receive a hundredfold more in this time, houses, and brethren, and sisters, and mothers, and children, and lands, with persecutions; and in the aye to come eternal life." (Mark x. 28–30.)

Jesus declared, it is true, that those who follow his doctrine must expect to be persecuted by those who do not follow it, but he did not say that his disciples will be the worse off for that reason; on the contrary, he said that his disciples would have, here, in this world, more benefits than those who did not follow him. That Jesus said and thought this is beyond a doubt, as the clearness of his words on this subject, the meaning of his entire doctrine, his life and the life of his disciples, plainly show. But was his teaching in this respect true?

When we examine the question as to which of the two conditions would be the better, that of the disciples of Jesus or that of the disciples of the world, we are obliged to conclude that the condition of the disciples of Jesus ought to be the most desirable, since the disciples of Jesus, in doing good to every one, would not arouse the hatred of men. The disciples of Jesus, doing evil to no one, would be persecuted only by the wicked. The disciples of the world, on the contrary, are likely to be persecuted by every one, since the law of the disciples of the world is the law of each for himself, the law of struggle; that is, of mutual persecution. Moreover, the disciples of Jesus would be prepared for suffering, while the disciples of the world use all possible means to avoid suffering; the disciples of Jesus would feel that their sufferings were useful to the world; but the disciples of the world do not know why they suffer. On abstract grounds, then, the condition of the disciples of Jesus would be more advantageous than that of the disciples of the world. But is it so in reality? To answer this, let each one call to mind all the painful moments of his life, all the physical and moral sufferings that he has endured, and let him ask himself if he has suffered these calamities in behalf of the doctrine of the world or in behalf of the doctrine of Jesus. Every sincere man will find in recalling his past life that he has never once suffered for practising the doctrine of Jesus. He will find that the greater part of the misfortunes of his life have resulted from following the doctrines of the world. In my own life (an exceptionally happy one from a worldly point of view) I can reckon up as much suffering caused by following the doctrine of the world as many a martyr has endured for the doctrine of Jesus. All the most painful moments of my life, the orgies and duels in which I took part as a student, the wars in which I have participated, the diseases that I have endured, and the abnormal and insupportable conditions under which I now live, all these are only so much martyrdom exacted by fidelity to the doctrine of the world. But I speak of a life exceptionally happy from a worldly point of view. How many martyrs have suffered for the doctrine of the world torments that I should find difficulty in enumerating!

"We do not realize the difficulties and dangers entailed by the practice of the doctrine of the world, simply because we are persuaded that we could not do otherwise than follow that doctrine. We are persuaded that all the calamities that we inflict upon ourselves are the result of the inevitable conditions of life, and we cannot understand that the doctrine of Jesus teaches us how we may rid ourselves of these calamities and render our lives happy. To be able to reply to the question, which of these two conditions is the happier? We must, at least for the time being, put aside our prejudices and take a careful survey of our surroundings.

Go through our great cities and observe the emaciated, sickly, and distorted specimens of humanity to be found therein; recall your own existence and that of all the people with whose lives you are familiar; recall the instances of violent deaths and suicides of which you have heard, and then ask yourself for what cause all this suffering and death, this despair that leads to suicide, has been endured. You will find, perhaps to your surprise, that nine-tenths of all human suffering endured by men is useless, and ought not to exist, that, in fact, the majority of men are martyrs to the doctrine of the world.

One rainy autumn day I rode on the tramway by the Sukhareff Tower in Moscow. For the distance of half a verst the vehicle forced its way through a compact crowd which quickly reformed its ranks. From morning till night these thousands of men, the greater portion of them starving and in rags, tramped angrily through the mud, venting their hatred in abusive epithets and acts of violence. The same sight may be seen in all the market places of Moscow. At sunset these people go to the taverns and gaming houses; their nights are passed in filth and wretchedness.

Think of the lives of these people, of what they abandon through choice for their present condition; think of the heavy burden of labor without reward which weighs upon these men and women, and you will see that they are true martyrs. All these people have forsaken houses, lands, parents, wives, and children; they have renounced all the comforts of life, and they have come to the cities to acquire that which according to the gospel of the world is indispensable to every one. And all these tens of thousands of unhappy people sleep in hovels, and subsist upon strong drink and wretched food. But aside from this class, all, from factory workman, cab driver, sewing girl, and lorette, to merchant and government official, all endure the most painful and abnormal conditions without being able to acquire what, according to the doctrine of the world, is indispensable to each.

Seek among all these men, from beggar to millionaire, one who is contented with his lot, and you will not find one such in a thousand. Each one spends his strength in pursuit of what is exacted by the doctrine of the world, and of what he is unhappy not to possess, and scarcely has he obtained one object of his desires when he strives for another, and still another, in that infinite labor of Sisyphus which destroys the lives of men. Run over the scale of individual fortunes, ranging from a yearly income of three hundred roubles to fifty thousand roubles, and you will rarely find a person who is not striving to gain four hundred roubles if he have three hundred, five hundred if he have four hundred, and so on to the top of the ladder. Among them all you will scarcely find one who, with five hundred roubles, is willing to adopt the mode of life of him who has only four hundred. When such an instance does occur, it is not inspired by a desire to make life more simple, but to amass money and make it more sure. Each strives continually to make the heavy burden of existence still heavier, by giving himself up body and soul to the practice of the doctrine of the world. Today we must buy an overcoat and galoches, tomorrow, a watch and chain; the next day we must install ourselves in an apartment with a sofa and a bronze lamp; then we must have carpets and velvet gowns; then a house, horses and carriages, paintings and decorations, and then we fall ill of overwork and die. Another continues the same task, sacrifices his life to this same Moloch, and then dies also, without realizing for what he has lived.

But possibly this existence is in itself attractive? Compare it with what men have always called happiness, and you will see that it is hideous. For what, according to the general estimate, are the principal conditions of earthly happiness? One of the first conditions of happiness is that the link between man and nature shall not be severed, that is, that he shall be able to see the sky above him, and that he shall be able to enjoy the sunshine, the pure air, the fields with their verdure, their multitudinous life. Men have always regarded it as a great unhappiness to be deprived of all these things. But what is the condition of those men who live according to the doctrine of the world? The greater their success in practising the doctrine of the world, the more they are deprived of these conditions of happiness. The greater their worldly success, the less they are able to enjoy the light of the sun, the freshness of the fields and woods, and all the delights of country life. Many of them – including nearly all the women – arrive at old age without having seen the sun rise or the beauties of the early morning, without having seen a forest except from a seat in a carriage, without ever having planted a field or a garden, and without having the least idea as to the ways and habits of dumb animals.

These people, surrounded by artificial light instead of sunshine, look only upon fabrics of tapes try and stone and wood fashioned by the hand of man; the roar of machinery, the roll of vehicles, the thunder of cannon, the sound of musical instruments, are always in their ears; they breathe an atmosphere heavy with distilled perfumes and tobacco smoke; because of the weakness of their stomachs and their depraved tastes they eat rich and highly spiced food. When they move about from place to place, they travel in closed carriages. When they go into the country, they have the same fabrics beneath their feet; the same draperies shut out the sunshine; and the same array of servants cut off all communication with the men, the earth, the vegetation, and the animals about them. Wherever they go, they are like so many captives shut out from the conditions of happiness. As prisoners sometimes console themselves with a blade of grass that forces its way through the pavement of their prison yard, or make pets of a spider or a mouse, so these people sometimes amuse themselves with sickly plants, a parrot, a poodle, or a monkey, to whose needs however they do not themselves administer.

Another inevitable condition of happiness is work: first, the intellectual labor that one is free to choose and loves; secondly, the exercise of physical power that brings a good appetite and tranquil and profound sleep. Here, again, the greater the imagined prosperity that falls to the lot of men according to the doctrine of the world, the more such men are deprived of this condition of happiness. All the prosperous people of the world, the men of dignity and wealth, are as completely deprived of the advantages of work as if they were shut up in solitary confinement. They struggle unsuccessfully with the diseases caused by the need of physical exercise, and with the ennui which pursues them unsuccessfully, because labor is a pleasure only when it is necessary, and they have need of nothing; or they undertake work that is odious to them, like the bankers, solicitors, administrators, and government officials, and their wives, who plan receptions and routs and devise toilettes for them selves and their children. (I say odious, because I never yet met any person of this class who was contented with his work or took as much satisfaction in it as the porter feels in shovelling away the snow from before their doorsteps.) All these favorites of fortune are either deprived of work or are obliged to work at what they do not like, after the manner of criminals condemned to hard labor.

The third undoubted condition of happiness is the family. But the more men are enslaved by worldly success, the more certainly are they cut off from domestic pleasures. The majority of them are libertines, who deliberately renounce the joys of family life and retain only its cares. If they are not libertines, their children, instead of being a source of pleasure, are a burden, and all possible means are employed to render marriage unfruitful. If they have children, they make no effort to cultivate the pleasures of companionship with them. They leave their children almost continually to the care of strangers, confiding them first to the instruction of persons who are usually foreigners, and then sending them to public educational institutions, so that of family life they have only the sorrows, and the children from infancy are as unhappy as their parents and wish their parents dead that they may become the heirs. These people are not confined in prisons, but the consequences of their way of living with regard to the family are more melancholy than the deprivation from the domestic relations inflicted upon those who are kept in confinement under sentence of the law.

The fourth condition of happiness is sympathetic and unrestricted intercourse with all classes of men. And the higher a man is placed in the social scale, the more certainly is he deprived of this essential condition of happiness. The higher he goes, the narrower becomes his circle of associates; the lower sinks the moral and intellectual level of those to whose companionship he is restrained.

The peasant and his wife are free to enter into friendly relations with everyone, and if a million men will have nothing to do with them, there remain eighty millions of people with whom they may fraternize, from Archangel to Astrakhan, without waiting for a ceremonious visit or an introduction. A clerk and his wife will find hundreds of people who are their equals; but the clerks of a higher rank will not admit them to a footing of social equality, and they, in their turn, are excluded by others. The wealthy man of the world reckons by dozens the families with whom he is willing to maintain social ties all the rest of the world are strangers. For the cabinet minister and the millionaire there are only a dozen people as rich and as important as themselves. For kings and emperors, the circle is still more narrow. Is not the whole system like a great prison where each inmate is restricted to association with a few fellow convicts?

Finally, the fifth condition of happiness is bodily health. And once more we find that as we ascend the social scale this condition of happiness is less and less within the reach of the followers of the doctrine of the world. Compare a family of medium social status with a family of peasants.

The latter toil unremittingly and are robust of body; the former is made up of men and women more or less subject to disease. Recall to mind the rich men and women whom you have known; are not most of them invalids? A person of that class whose physical disabilities do not oblige him to take a periodical course of hygienic and medical treatment is as rare as is an invalid among the laboring classes. All these favorites of fortune are the victims and practitioners of sexual vices that have become a second nature, and they are toothless, gray, and bald at an age when a workingman is in the prime of manhood. Nearly all are afflicted with nervous or other diseases arising from excesses in eating, drunkenness, luxury, and perpetual medication. Those who do not die young, pass half of their lives under the influence of morphine or other drugs, as melancholy wrecks of humanity incapable of self-attention, leading a parasitic existence like that of a certain species of ants which are nourished by their slaves. Here is the death list. One has blown out his brains, another has rotted away from the effects of syphilitic poison; this old man succumbed to sexual excesses, this young man to a wild outburst of sensuality; one died of drunkenness, another of gluttony, another from the abuse of morphine, another from an induced abortion. One after another they perished, victims of the doctrine of the world. And a multitude presses on behind them, like an army of martyrs, to undergo the same sufferings, the same perdition.

To follow the doctrine of Jesus is difficult! Jesus said that they who would forsake houses, and lands, and brethren, and follow his doctrine should receive a hundred-fold in houses, and lands, and brethren, and besides all this, eternal life. And no one is willing even to make the experiment. The doctrine of the world commands its followers to leave houses, and lands, and brethren; to forsake the country for the filth of the city, there to toil as a bath-keeper soaping the backs of others; as an apprentice in a little underground shop passing life in counting kopecks; as a prosecuting attorney to serve in bringing unhappy wretches under condemnation of the law; as a cabinet minister, perpetually signing documents of no importance; as the head of an army, killing men. "Forsake all and live this hideous life ending in a cruel death, and you shall receive nothing in this world or the other," is the command, and every one listens and obeys. Jesus tells us to take up the cross and follow him, to bear submissively the lot apportioned out to us. No one hears his words or follows his command. But let a man in a uniform decked out with gold lace, a man whose speciality is to kill his fellows, say, "Take, not your cross, but your knapsack and carbine, and march to suffering and certain death," and a mighty host is ready to receive his orders. Leaving parents, wives, and children, clad in grotesque costumes, subject to the will of the first comer of a higher rank, famished, benumbed, and exhausted by forced marches, they go, like a herd of cattle to the slaughterhouse, not knowing where, and yet these are not cattle, they are men. With despair in their hearts they move on, to die of hunger, or cold, or disease, or, if they survive, to be brought within range of a storm of bullets and commanded to kill. They kill and are killed, none of them knows why or to what end. An ambitious stripling has only to brandish his sword and shout a few magniloquent words to induce them to rush to certain death. And yet no one finds this to be difficult. Neither the victims, nor those whom they have forsaken, find anything difficult in such sacrifices, in which parents encourage their children to take part. It seems to them not only that such things should be, but that they could not be otherwise, and that they are altogether admirable and moral.

If the practice of the doctrine of the world were easy, agreeable, and without danger, we might per haps believe that the practice of the doctrine of Jesus is difficult, frightful, and cruel. But the doctrine of the world is much more difficult, more dangerous, and more cruel, than is the doctrine of Jesus. Formerly, we are told, there were martyrs for the cause of Jesus; but they were exceptional. We cannot count up more than about three hundred and eighty thousand of them, voluntary and involuntary, in the whole course of eighteen hundred years; but who shall count the martyrs to the doctrine of the world? For each Christian martyr there have been a thousand martyrs to the doctrine of the world, and the sufferings of each one of them have been a hundred times more cruel than those endured by the others. The number of the victims of wars in our century alone amounts to thirty millions of men. These are the martyrs to the doctrine of the world, who would have escaped suffering and death even if they had refused to follow the doctrine of the world, to say nothing of following the doctrine of Jesus.

If a man will cease to have faith in the doctrine of the world and not think it indispensable to wear varnished boots and a gold chain, to maintain a useless salon, or to do the various other foolish things the doctrine of the world demands, he will never know the effects of brutalizing occupations, of unlimited suffering, of the anxieties of a perpetual struggle; he will remain in communion with nature; he will be deprived neither of the work he loves, or of his family, or of his health, and he will not perish by a cruel and brutish death.

The doctrine of Jesus does not exact martyrdom similar to that of the doctrine of the world; it teaches us rather how to put an end to the sufferings that men endure in the name of the false doctrine of the world. The doctrine of Jesus has a profound metaphysical meaning; it has a meaning as an expression of the aspirations of humanity; but it has also for each individual a very simple, very clear, and very practical meaning with regard to the conduct of his own life. In fact, we might say that Jesus taught men not to do foolish things.

The meaning of the doctrine of Jesus is simple and accessible to all.

Jesus said that we were not to be angry, and not to consider ourselves as better than others; if we were angry and offended others, so much the worse for us. Again, he said that we were to avoid libertinism, and to that end choose one woman, to whom we should remain faithful. Once more, he said that we were not to bind ourselves by promises or oaths to the service of those who may constrain us to commit acts of folly and wickedness. Then he said that we were not to return evil for evil, lest the evil rebound upon ourselves with redoubled force. And, finally, he says that we are not to consider men as foreigners because they dwell in another country and speak a language different from our own. And the conclusion is, that if we avoid doing any of these foolish things, we shall be happy.

This is all very well (we say,) but the world is so organized that, if we place ourselves in opposition to it, our condition will be much more calamitous than if we live in accordance with its doctrine. If a man refuses to perform military service, he will be shut up in a fortress, and possibly will be shot. If a man will not do what is necessary for the support of himself and his family, he and his family will starve. Thus argue the people who feel them selves obliged to defend the existing social organization; but they do not believe in the truth of their own words. They only say this because they can not deny the truth of the doctrine of Jesus which they profess, and because they must justify them selves in some way for their failure to practise it. They not only do not believe in what they say; they have never given any serious consideration to the subject. They have faith in the doctrine of the world, and they only make use of the plea they have learned from the Church, that much suffering is inevitable for those who would practise the doctrine of Jesus; and so they have never tried to practise the doctrine of Jesus at all.

We see enough of the frightful suffering endured by men in following the doctrine of the world, but in these times we hear nothing of suffering in behalf of the doctrine of Jesus. Thirty millions of men have perished in wars, fought in behalf of the doctrine of the world; thousands of millions of beings have perished, crushed by a social system organized on the principle of the doctrine of the world; but where, in our day, shall we find a million, a thousand, a dozen, or a single one, who has died a cruel death, or has even suffered from hunger and cold, in behalf of the doctrine of Jesus? This fear of suffering is only a puerile excuse that proves how little we really know of Jesus doctrine. We not only do not follow it; we do not even take it seriously. The Church has explained it in such a way that it seems to be, not the doctrine of a happy life, but a bugbear, a source of terror.

Jesus calls men to drink of a well of living water, which is free to all. Men are parched with thirst, they have eaten of filth and drunk blood, but they have been told that they will perish if they drink of this water that is offered them by Jesus, and men believe in the warnings of superstition. They die in torment, with the water that they dare not touch within their reach. If they would only have faith in Jesus words, and go to this well of living water and quench their thirst, they would realize how cunning has been the imposture practised upon them by the Church, and how needlessly their sufferings have been prolonged. If they would only accept the doctrine of Jesus, frankly and simply, they would see at once the horrible error of which we are each and all the victims.

One generation after another strives to find the security of its existence in violence, and by violence to protect its privileges. "We believe that the happiness of our life is in power, and domination, and abundance of worldly goods. We are so habituated to this idea that we are alarmed at the sacrifices exacted by the doctrine of Jesus, which teaches that man's happiness does not depend upon fortune and power, and that the rich cannot enter into the kingdom of God. But this is a false idea of the doctrine of Jesus, which teaches us, not to do what is the worst, but to do what is the best for ourselves here in this present life. Inspired by his love for men, Jesus taught them not to depend upon a security based upon violence, and not to seek after riches, just as we teach the common people to abstain, for their own interest, from quarrels and intemperance. He said that if men lived without defending themselves against violence, and without possessing riches, they would be more happy; and he confirms his words by the example of his life. He said that a man who lives according to his doctrine must be ready at any moment to endure violence from others, and, possibly, to die of hunger and cold. But this warning, which seems to exact such great and unbearable sacrifices, is simply a statement of the conditions under which men always have existed, and always will continue to exist.

A disciple of Jesus should be prepared for everything, and especially for suffering and death. But is the disciple of the world in a more desirable situation? We are so accustomed to believe in all we do for the so-called security of life (the organization of armies, the building of fortresses, the provisioning of troops), that our wardrobes, our systems of medical treatment, our furniture, and our money, all seem like real and stable pledges of our existence. We forget the fate of him who resolved to build greater storehouses to provide an abundance for many years: he died in a night. Everything that we do to make our existence secure is like the act of the ostrich, when she hides her head in the sand, and does not see that her destruction is near. But we are even more foolish than the ostrich. To establish the doubtful security of an uncertain life in an uncertain future, we sacrifice a life of certainty in a present that we might really possess.

The illusion is in the firm conviction that our existence can be made secure by a struggle with others.

"We are so accustomed to this illusory so-called security of our existence and our property, that we do not realize what we lose by striving after it. We lose everything, we lose life itself. Our whole life is taken up with anxiety for personal security, with preparations for living, so that we really never live at all.

If we take a general survey of our lives, we shall see that all our efforts in behalf of the so-called security of existence are not made at all for the assurance of security, but simply to help us to forget that existence never has been, and never can be, secure. But it is not enough to say that we are the dupes of our own illusions, and that we forfeit the true life for an imaginary life; our efforts for security often result in the destruction of what we most wish to preserve. The French took up arms in 1870 to make their national existence secure, and the attempt resulted in the destruction of hundreds of thousands of Frenchmen. All people who take up arms undergo the same experience. The rich man believes that his existence is secure because he possesses money, and his money attracts a thief who kills him. The invalid thinks to make his life secure by the use of medicines, and the medicines slowly poison him; if they do not bring about his death, they at least deprive him of life, till he is like the impotent man who waited thirty-five years at the pool for an angel to come down and trouble the waters. The doctrine of Jesus, which teaches us that we cannot possibly make life secure, but that we must be ready to die at any moment, is unquestionably preferable to the doctrine of the world, which obliges us to struggle for the security of existence. It is preferable because the impossibility of escaping death, and the impossibility of making life secure, is the same for the disciples of Jesus as it is for the disciples of the world; but, according to the doctrine of Jesus, life itself is not absorbed in the idle attempt to make existence secure. To the follower of Jesus life is free, and can be devoted to the end for which it is worthy, its own welfare and the welfare of others. The disciple of Jesus will be poor, but that is only saying that he will always enjoy the gifts that God has lavished upon men. He will not ruin his own existence. We make the word poverty a synonym for calamity, but it is in truth a source of happiness, and however much we may regard it as a calamity, it remains a source of happiness still. To be poor means not to live in cities, but in the country, not to be shut up in close rooms, but to labor out of doors, in the woods and fields, to have the delights of sunshine, of the open heavens, of the earth, of observing the habits of dumb animals; not to rack our brains with inventing dishes to stimulate an appetite, and not to endure the pangs of indigestion. To be poor is to be hungry three times a day, to sleep without passing hours tossing upon the pillow a victim of insomnia, to have children, and have them always with us, to do nothing that we do not wish to do (this is essential), and to have no fear for anything that may happen. The poor person will be ill and will suffer; he will die like the rest of the world; but his sufferings and his death will probably be less painful than those of the rich; and he will certainly live more happily. Poverty is one of the conditions of following the doctrine of Jesus, a condition indispensable to those who would enter into the kingdom of God and be happy.

The objection to this is, that no one will care for us, and that we shall be left to die of hunger. To this objection we may reply in the words of Jesus, (words that have been interpreted to justify the idleness of the clergy)

"Get you no gold, nor silver, nor brass in your purses; no wallet for your journey, neither two coats, nor shoes, nor staff: for the laborer is worthy of his food" (Matt. x. 10).

"And into whatsoever house ye shall enter, . . . in that same house remain, eating and drinking such things as they give: for the laborer is worthy of his hire" (Luke x. 5, 7).

The laborer is worthy of ($A\xi\iota\acute{o}\varsigma$ $\varepsilon\sigma\tau\iota\nu$ means, word for word, can and ought to have) his food. It is a very short sentence, but he who understands it as Jesus understood it, will no longer have any fear of dying of hunger. To understand the true meaning of these words we must get rid of that traditional idea which we have developed from the doctrine of the redemption that man's felicity consists in idleness. "We must get back to that point of view natural to all men who are not fallen, that work, and not idleness, is the indispensable condition of happiness for every human being; that man cannot, in fact, refrain from work. We must rid ourselves of the savage prejudice which leads us to think that a man who has an income from a place under the government, from landed property, or from stocks and bonds, is in a natural and happy position because he is relieved from the necessity of work. We must get back into the human brain the idea of work possessed by undegenerate men, the idea that Jesus has, when he says that the laborer is worthy of his food. Jesus did not imagine that men would regard work as a curse, and consequently he did not have in mind a man who would not work, or desired not to work. He supposed that all his disciples would work, and so he said that if a man would work, his work would bring him food. He who makes use of the labor of another will provide food for him who labors, simply because he profits by that labor. And so he who works will always have food; he may not have property, but as to food, there need be no uncertainty whatever.

With regard to work there is a difference between the doctrine of Jesus and the doctrine of the world. According to the doctrine of the world, it is very meritorious in a man to be willing to work; he is thereby enabled to enter into competition with others, and to demand wages proportionate to his qualifications. According to the doctrine of Jesus, labor is the inevitable condition of human life, and food is the inevitable consequence of labor.

Labor produces food, and food produces labor. However cruel and grasping the employer may be, he will always feed his workman, as he will always feed his horse; he feeds him that he may get all the work possible, and in this way he contributes to the welfare of the workman.

"For verily the Son of man came not to be ministered unto, but to minister and to give his life a ransom for many."

According to the doctrine of Jesus, every individual will be the happier the more clearly he understands that his vocation consists, not in exacting service from others, but in ministering to others, in giving his life for the ransom of many. A man who does this will be worthy of his food and will not fail to have it. By the words, "came not to be ministered unto but to minister," Jesus established a method which would insure the material existence of man; and by the words, "the laborer is worthy of his food," he answered once for all the objection that a man who should practise the doctrine of Jesus in the midst of those who do not practise it would be in danger of perishing from hunger and cold. Jesus practised his own doctrine amid great opposition, and he did not perish from hunger and cold. He showed that a man does not insure his own subsistence by amassing worldly goods at the expense of others, but by rendering himself useful and indispensable to others. The more necessary he is to others, the more will his existence be made secure.

There are in the world as it is now organized millions of men who possess no property and do not practise the doctrine of Jesus by ministering unto others, but they do not die of hunger. How, then, can we object to the doctrine of Jesus, that those who practise it by working for others will perish for want of food? Men cannot die of hunger while the rich have bread. In Russia there are millions of men who possess nothing and subsist entirely by their own toil. The existence of a Christian would be as secure among pagans as it would be among those of his own faith. He would labor for others; he would be necessary to them, and therefore he would be fed. Even a dog, if be useful, is fed and cared for; and shall not a man be fed and cared for whose service is necessary to the whole world?

But those who seek by all possible means to justify the personal life have another objection. They say that if a man be sick, even if he have a wife, parents, and children dependent upon him, if this man cannot work, he will not be fed. They say so, and they will continue to say so; but their own actions prove that they do not believe what they say. These same people who will not admit that the doctrine of Jesus is practicable, practise it to a certain extent themselves. They do not cease to care for a sick sheep, a sick ox, or a sick dog. They do not kill an old horse, but they give him work in proportion to his strength. They care for all sorts of animals without expecting any benefit in return; and can it be that they will not care for a useful man who has fallen sick, that they will not find work suited to the strength of the old man and the child, that they will not care for the very babes who later on will be able to work for them in re turn? As a matter of fact they do all this. Nine-tenths of men are cared for by the other tenth, like so many cattle. And however great the darkness in which this one-tenth live, however mistaken their views in regard to the other nine-tenths of humanity, the tenth, even if they had the power, would not deprive the other nine-tenths of food.

The rich will not deprive the poor of what is necessary, because they wish them to multiply and work, and so in these days the little minority of rich people provide directly or indirectly for the nourishment of the majority, that the latter may furnish the maximum of work, and multiply, and bring up a new supply of workers. Ants care for the increase and welfare of their slaves. Shall not men care for those whose labor they find necessary? Laborers are necessary. And those who profit by labor will always be careful to provide the means of labor for those who are willing to work.

The objection concerning the possibility of practising the doctrine of Jesus, that if men do not acquire something for themselves and have wealth in reserve no one will take care of their families, is true, but it is true only in regard to idle and use less and obnoxious people such as make up the majority of our opulent classes. No one (with the exception of foolish parents) takes the trouble to care for lazy people, because lazy people are of no use to anyone, not even to themselves; as for the workers, the most selfish and cruel of men will contribute to their welfare. People breed and train and care for oxen, and a man, as a beast of burden, is much more useful than an ox, as the tariff of the slave-mart shows. This is why children will never be left without support.

Man is not in the world to work for himself; he is in the world to work for others, and the laborer is worthy of his hire. These truths are justified by universal experience; now, always, and everywhere, the man who labors receives the means of bodily subsistence. This subsistence is assured to him who works against his will; for such a work man desires only to relieve himself of the necessity of work, and acquires all that he possibly can in order that he may take the yoke from his own neck and place it upon the neck of another. A workman like this envious, grasping, toiling against his will never lack for food and will be happier than one, who without labor, lives upon the labor of others. How much more happy, then, will that laborer be who labors in obedience to the doctrine of Jesus with the object of accomplishing all the work of which he is capable and wishing for it the least possible return? How much more desirable will his condition be, as, little by little, he sees his example followed by others. For services rendered he will then be the recipient of equal services in return.

The doctrine of Jesus with regard to labor and the fruits of labor is expressed in the story of the loaves and fishes, wherein it was shown that man enjoys the greatest sum of the benefits accessible to humanity, not by appropriating all that he can possibly grasp and using what he has for his personal pleasure, but by administering to the needs of others, as Jesus did by the borders of Galilee.

There were several thousand men and women to be fed. One of the disciples told Jesus that there was a lad who had five loaves and two fishes. Jesus understood that some of the people coming from a distance had brought provisions with them and that some had not, for after all were filled, the disciples gathered up twelve baskets full of fragments. (If no one but the boy had brought anything, how could so much have been left after so many were fed?) If Jesus had not set them an example, the people would have acted as people of the world act now. Some of those who had food would have eaten all that they had through gluttony or avidity, and some, after eating what they could eat, would have taken the rest to their homes. Those who had nothing would have been famished, and would have regarded their more fortunate companions with envy and hatred; some of them would perhaps have tried to take food by force from them who had it, and so hunger and anger and quarrels would have been the result. That is, the multitude would have acted just as people act nowadays.

But Jesus knew exactly what to do. He asked that all be made to sit down, and then commanded his disciples to give of what they had to those who had nothing, and to request others to do the same. The result was that those who had food followed the example of Jesus and his disciples, and offered what they had to others. Every one ate and was satisfied, and with the broken pieces that remained the disciples filled twelve baskets.

Jesus teaches every man to govern his life by the law of reason and conscience, for the law of reason is as applicable to the individual as it is to humanity at large. Work is the inevitable condition of human life, the true source of human welfare. For this reason a refusal to divide the fruits of one's labor with others is a refusal to accept the conditions of true happiness. To give of the fruits of one's labor to others is to contribute to the welfare of all men. The retort is made that if men did not wrest food from others, they would die of hunger. To me it seems more reasonable to say, that if men do wrest their food from one another, some of them will die of hunger, and experience confirms this view.

Every man, whether he lives according to the doctrine of Jesus or according to the doctrine of the world, lives only by the sufferance and care of others. From his birth, man is cared for and nourished by others. According to the doctrine of the world, man has a right to demand that others should continue to nourish and care for him and for his family, but, according to the doctrine of Jesus, he is only entitled to care and nourishment on the condition that he do all he can for the service of others, and so render himself useful and indispensable to man kind. Men who live according to the doctrine of the world are usually anxious to rid themselves of anyone who is useless and whom they are obliged to feed; at the first possible opportunity they cease to feed such a one, and leave him to die, because of his uselessness; but him who lives for others according to the doctrine of Jesus, all men, however wicked they may be, will always nourish and care for, that he may continue to labor in their behalf.

Which, then, is the more reasonable; which offers the more joy and the greater security, a life according to the doctrine of the world, or a life according to the doctrine of Jesus?

Chapter 11

THE DOCTRINE OF JESUS is to bring the kingdom of God upon earth. The practice of this doctrine is not difficult; and not only so, its practice is a natural expression of the belief of all who recognize its truth. The doctrine of Jesus offers the only possible chance of salvation for those who would escape the perdition that threatens the personal life. The fulfilment of this doctrine not only will deliver men from the privations and sufferings of this life, but will put an end to nine-tenths of the suffering: endured in behalf of the doctrine of the world.

When I understood this I asked myself why I had never practised a doctrine which would give me so much happiness and peace and joy; why, on the other hand, I always had practised an entirely different doctrine, and thereby made myself wretched? Why? The reply was a simple one. Because I never had known the truth. The truth had been concealed from me.

When the doctrine of Jesus was first revealed to me, I did not believe that the discovery would lead me to reject the doctrine of the Church. I dreaded this separation, and in the course of my studies I did not attempt to search out the errors in the doctrine of the Church. 1 sought, rather, to close my eyes to propositions that seemed to be obscure and strange, provided they were not in evident contra diction with what I regarded as the substance of the Christian doctrine.

But the further I advanced in the study of the Gospels, and the more clearly the doctrine of Jesus was revealed to me, the more inevitable the choice became. I must either accept the doctrine of Jesus, a reasonable and simple doctrine in accordance with my conscience and my hope of salvation; or I must accept an entirely different doctrine, a doctrine in opposition to reason and conscience and that offered me nothing except the certainty of my own perdition and that of others. I was therefore forced to reject, one after another, the dogmas of the Church. This I did against my will, struggling with the desire to mitigate as much as possible my disagreement with the Church, that I might not be obliged to separate from the Church, and thereby deprive myself of communion with fellow believers, the greatest happiness that religion can bestow. But when I had completed my task, I saw that in spite of all my efforts to maintain a connecting link with the Church, the separation was complete. I knew before that the bond of union, if it existed at all, must be a very slight one, but I was soon convinced that it did not exist at all.

My son came to me one day, after I had completed my examination of the Gospels, and told me of a discussion that was going on between two domestics (uneducated persons who scarcely knew how to read) concerning a passage in some religious book which maintained that it was not a sin to put criminals to death, or to kill enemies in war. I could not believe that an assertion of this sort could be printed in any book, and I asked to see it. The volume bore the title of *A Book of Selected Prayers* (third edition; eighth ten thousand; Moscow: 1879). On page 163 of this book I read:

"What is the sixth commandment of God?" "Thou shalt not kill."

"What does God forbid by this commandment?" "He forbids us to kill, to take the life of any man. Is it a sin to punish a criminal with death according to the law, or to kill an enemy in war?"

"No; that is not a sin. We take the life of the criminal to put an end to the wrong that he commits; we slay an enemy in war, because in war we fight for our sovereign and our native land."

And in this manner was enjoined the abrogation of the law of God! I could scarcely believe that I had read aright.

My opinion was asked with regard to the subject at issue. To the one who maintained that the instruction given by the book was true, I said that the explanation was not correct.

"Why, then, do they print untrue explanations contrary to the law?" was his question, to which I could say nothing in reply.

I kept the volume and looked over its contents. The book contained thirty-one prayers with instructions concerning genuflexions and the joining of the fingers; an explanation of the Credo; a citation from the fifth chapter of Matthew without any explanation whatever, but headed, "Commands for those who would possess the Beatitudes "; the Ten Commandments accompanied by comments that rendered most of them void; and hymns for every saint's day.

As I have said, I not only had sought to avoid censure of the religion of the Church I had done my best to see only its most favorable side; and knowing its academic literature from beginning to end, I had paid no attention whatever to its popular literature. This book of devotion, spread broadcast in an enormous number of copies, awakening doubts in the minds of the most unlearned people, set me to thinking. The contents of the book seemed to me so entirely pagan, so wholly out of accord with Christianity, that I could not believe it to be the deliberate purpose of the Church to propagate such a doctrine. To verify my belief, I bought and read all the books published by the synod with its "benediction" (*blagoslovnia*), containing brief expositions of the religion of the Church for the use of children and the common people.

Their contents were to me almost entirely new, for at the time when I received my early religious instruction, they had not yet appeared. As far as I could remember there were no commandments with regard to the beatitudes, and there was no doctrine which taught that it was not a sin to kill. No such teachings appeared in the old catechisms; they were not to be found in the catechism of Peter Mogilas, or in that of Beliokof, or the abridged Catholic catechisms. The innovation was introduced by the metropolitan Philaret, who prepared a catechism with proper regard for the susceptibilities of the military class, and from this catechism the *Book of Selected Prayers* was compiled. Philaret's work is entitled, *The Christian Catechism of the Orthodox Church*, for the *Use of all Orthodox Christians*, and is published, "by order of his Imperial Majesty."

The book is divided into three parts, "Concerning Faith," "Concerning Hope," and "Concerning Love." The first part contains the analysis of the symbol of faith as given by the Council of Nice. The second part is made up of an exposition of the *Pater Noster*, and the first eight verses of the fifth chapter of Matthew, which serve as an introduction to the Sermon on the Mount, and are called (I know not why) "Commands for those who would possess the Beatitudes." These first two parts treat of the dogmas of the Church, prayers, and the sacraments, but they contain no rules with regard to the conduct of life. The third part, "Concerning Love," contains an exposition of Christian duties, based not on the commandments of Jesus, but upon the ten commandments of Moses. This exposition of the commandments of Moses seems to have been made for the" especial purpose of teaching men not to obey them. Each commandment is followed by a reservation which completely destroys it force. With regard to the first commandment, which enjoins the worship of God alone, the catechism inculcates the worship of saints and angels, to say nothing of the Mother of God and the three persons of the Trinity (*Special Catechism*, pp. 107, 108). With regard to the second commandment, against the worship of idols, the catechism enjoins the worship of images (p. 108). With regard to the third commandment, the catechism enjoins the taking of oaths as the principal token of legitimate authority (p. 111). With regard to the fourth commandment, concerning the observance of the Sabbath, the catechism inculcates the observance of Sunday, of the thirteen principal feasts, of a number of feasts of less importance, the observance of Lent, and of fasts on Wednesdays and Fridays (pp. 112–115). With regard to the fifth commandment, *"Honor thy father and thy mother"* the catechism prescribes honor to the sovereign, the country, spiritual fathers, all per sons in authority, and of these last gives an enumeration in three pages, including college authorities, civil, judicial, and military authorities, and owners of serfs, with instructions as to the manner of honoring each of these classes (pp. 116–119). My citations are taken from the sixty-fourth edition of the catechism, dated 1880. Twenty years have passed since the abolition of serfdom, and no one has taken the trouble to strike out the phrase which, in connection with the commandment of God to honor parents, was introduced into the catechism to sustain and justify slavery.

With regard to the sixth commandment, *"Thou shalt not kill,"* the instructions of the catechism are from the first in favor of murder.

"Question What does the sixth commandment forbid?

"Answer It forbids manslaughter, to take the life of one's neighbor in any manner whatever.

"*Question* Is all manslaughter a transgression of the law?

"*Answer* Manslaughter is not a transgression of the law when life is taken in pursuance of its mandate. For example:

"1st When a criminal condemned in justice is punished by death."

"2nd When we kill in war for the sovereign and our country."

The italics are in the original. Further on we read:

"*Question* With regard to manslaughter, when is the law transgressed?

* *Answer* When anyone conceals a murderer or sets him at liberty" (sic).

All this is printed in hundreds of thousands of copies, and under the name of Christian doctrine is taught by compulsion to every Russian, who is obliged to receive it under penalty of castigation. This is taught to all the Russian people. It is taught to the innocent children, to the children whom Jesus commanded to be brought to him as belonging to the kingdom of God; to the children whom we must resemble, in ignorance of false doctrines, to enter into the kingdom of God; to the children whom Jesus tried to protect in proclaiming woe on him who should cause one of the little ones to stumble! And the little children are obliged to learn all this, and are told that it is the only and sacred law of God. These are not proclamations sent out clandestinely, whose authors are punished with penal servitude; they are proclamations which inflict the punishment of penal servitude upon all those who do not agree with the doctrines they inculcate.

As I write these lines, I experience a feeling of insecurity, simply because I have allowed myself to say that men cannot render void the fundamental law of God inscribed in all the codes and in all hearts, by such words as these:

"Manslaughter is not a transgression of the law when life is taken in pursuance of its mandate, when we kill in war for our sovereign and our country."

I tremble because I have allowed myself to say that such things should not be taught to children.

It was against such teachings as these that Jesus warned men when he said:

"Look, therefore, whether the light that is in thee be not darkness." (Luke xi. 35.)

The light that is in us has become darkness; and the darkness of our lives is full of terror.

"Woe unto you, scribes and Pharisees, hypocrites because ye shut the kingdom of heaven against men: for ye enter not in yourselves, neither suffer ye them that are entering in to enter. Woe unto you, scribes and Pharisees, hypocrites! for ye devour widows houses, even while for a pretence ye make long prayers: therefore ye shall receive greater condemnation. Woe unto you, scribes and Pharisees, hypocrites! for ye compass sea and land to make one proselyte; and when he is become so, ye make him twofold more a son of hell than yourselves. Woe unto you, ye blind guides.

"Woe unto you, scribes and Pharisees, hypocrites! For ye build the sepulchres of the prophets, and garnish the tombs of the righteous, and say, if we had been in the days of our fathers, we should not have been partakers with them in the blood of the prophets. Wherefore ye witness to yourselves, that ye are sons of them that slew the prophets. Fill ye up, then, the measure of your fathers. I send unto you prophets, and wise men, and scribes: some of them shall ye kill and crucify; and some of them shall ye scourge in your synagogues, and persecute from city to city: that upon you may come all the righteous blood shed on the earth, from the blood of Abel.

"Every sin and blasphemy shall be forgiven unto men; but the blasphemy against the Spirit shall not be forgiven."

Of a truth we might say that all this was written but yesterday, not against men who no longer compass sea and land to blaspheme against the Spirit, or to convert men to a religion that renders its proselytes worse than they were before, but against men who deliberately force people to embrace their religion, and persecute and bring to death all the prophets and the righteous who seek to reveal their falsehoods to mankind. I became convinced that the doctrine of the Church, although bearing the name of "Christian," is one with the darkness against which Jesus struggled, and against which he commanded his disciples to strive.

The doctrine of Jesus, like all religious doctrines, is "regarded in two ways, first, as a moral and ethical system which teaches men how they should live as individuals, and in relation to each other; second, as a metaphysical theory which explains why men should live in a given manner and not otherwise. One necessitates the other. Man should live in this manner because such is his destiny; or, man's destiny is this way, and consequently he should follow it. These two methods of doctrinal expression are common to all the religions of the world, to the religion of the Brahmins, to that of Confucius, to that of Buddha, to that of Moses, and to that of the Christ. But, with regard to the doctrine of Jesus, as with regard to all other doctrines, men wander from its precepts, and they always find someone to justify their deviations. Those who, as Jesus said, sit in Moses' seat, explain the metaphysical theory in such a way that the ethical prescriptions of the doctrine cease to be regarded as obligatory, and are replaced by external forms of worship, by ceremonial. This is a condition common to all religions, but, to me, it seems that it never has been manifested with so much pomp as in connection with Christianity, and for two reasons: first, because the doctrine of Jesus is the most elevated of all doctrines (the most elevated because the metaphysical and ethical portions are so closely united that one cannot be separated from the other without destroying the vitality of the whole); second, because the doctrine of Jesus is in itself a protest against all forms, a negation not only of Jewish ceremonial, but of all exterior rites of worship. Therefore, the arbitrary separation of the metaphysical and ethical aspects of Christianity entirely disfigures the doctrine, and deprives it of every sort of meaning. The separation began with the preaching of Paul, who knew but imperfectly the ethical doctrine set forth in the Gospel of Matthew, and who preached a meta-physico-cabalistic theory entirely foreign to the doctrine of Jesus; and this theory was perfected under Constantine, when the existing pagan social organization was proclaimed Christian simply by covering it with the mantle of Christianity. After Constantine, that arch pagan, whom the Church in spite of all his crimes and vices admits to the category of the saints, after Constantine began the domination of the councils, and the centre of gravity of Christianity was permanently displaced till only the metaphysical portion was left in view. And this metaphysical theory with its accompanying ceremonial deviated more and more from its true and primitive meaning, until it has reached its present stage of development, as a doctrine which explains the mysteries of a celestial life beyond the comprehension of human reason, and, with all its complicated formulas, gives no religious guidance whatever with regard to the regulation of this earthly life.

All religious, with the exception of the religion of the Christian Church, demand from their adherents aside from forms and ceremonies, the practice of certain actions called good, and abstinence from certain actions that are called bad. The Jewish religion prescribed circumcision, the observance of the Sabbath, the giving of alms, the feast of the Passover. Mohammedanism prescribes circumcision, prayer five times a day, the giving of tithes to the poor, pilgrimage to the tomb of the Prophet, and many other things. It is the same with all other religions. Whether these prescriptions are good or bad, they are prescriptions which exact the performance of certain actions. Pseudo-Christianity alone prescribes nothing. There is nothing that a Christian is obliged to observe except fasts and prayers, which the Church itself does not recognize as obligatory. All that is necessary to the pseudo-Christian is the sacrament. But the sacrament is not fulfilled by the believer; it is administered to him by others. The pseudo-Christian is obliged to do nothing or to abstain from nothing for his own salvation, since the Church administers to him everything of which he has need. The Church baptizes him, anoints him, gives him the eucharist, confesses him, even after he has lost consciousness, administers extreme unction to him, and prays for him, and he is saved. From the time of Constantine the Christian Church has prescribed no religious duties to its adherents. It has never required that they should abstain from anything. The Christian Church has recognized and sanctioned divorce, slavery, tribunals, all earthly powers, the death penalty, and war; it has exacted nothing except a renunciation of a purpose to do evil on the occasion of baptism, and this only in its early days: later on, when infant baptism was introduced, even this requirement was no longer observed.

The Church confesses the doctrine of Jesus in theory, but denies it in practice. Instead of guiding the life of the world, the Church, through affection for the world, expounds the metaphysical doctrine of Jesus in such a way as not to derive from it any obligation as to the conduct of life, any necessity for men to live differently from the way in which they have been living. The Church has surrendered to the world, and simply follows in the train of its victor. The world does as it pleases, and leaves to the Church the task of justifying its actions with explanations as to the meaning of life. The world organizes an existence in absolute opposition to the doctrine of Jesus, and the Church endeavors to demonstrate that men who live contrary to the doctrine of Jesus really live in accordance with that doctrine. The final result is that the world lives a worse than pagan existence, and the Church not only approves, but maintains that this existence is in exact conformity to the doctrine of Jesus.

But a time comes when the light of the true doctrine of Jesus shines forth from the Gospels, not withstanding the guilty efforts of the Church to conceal it from men's eyes, as, for instance, in prohibiting the translation of the Bible; there comes a time when the light reaches the people, even through the medium of sectarians and free-thinkers, and the falsity of the doctrine of the Church is shown so clearly that men begin to transform the method of living that the Church has justified.

Thus men of their own accord, and in opposition to the sanction of the Church, have abolished slavery, abolished the divine right of emperors and popes, and are now proceeding to abolish property and the State. And the Church cannot forbid such action because the abolition of these iniquities is in conformity to the Christian doctrine, that the Church preaches after having falsified.

And in this way the conduct of human life is freed from the control of the Church, and subjected to an entirely different authority. The Church retains its dogmas, but what are its dogmas worth? A metaphysical explanation can be of use only when there is a doctrine of life which it serves to make manifest. But the Church possesses only the explanation of an organization which it once sanctioned, and which no longer exists. The

Church has nothing left but temples and shrines and canonicals and vestments and words.

For eighteen centuries the Church has hidden the light of Christianity behind its forms and ceremonials, and by this same light it is put to shame.

The world, with an organization sanctioned by the Church, has rejected the Church in the name of the very principles of Christianity that the Church has professed. The separation between the two is complete and cannot be concealed. Everything that truly lives in the world of Europe today (everything not cold and dumb in hateful isolation), everything that is living, is detached from the Church, from all churches, and has an existence independent of the Church. Let it not be said that this is true only of the decayed civilizations of Western Europe. Russia, with its millions of civilized and uncivilized Christian rationalists, who have rejected the doctrine of the Church, proves incontestably that as regards emancipation from the yoke of the Church, she is, thanks be to God, in a worse condition of decay than the rest of Europe.

All that lives is independent of the Church. The power of the State is based upon tradition, upon science, upon popular suffrage, upon brute force, upon everything except upon the Church. Wars, the relation of State with State, are governed by principles of nationality, of the balance of power, but not by the Church. The institutions established by the State frankly ignore the Church. The idea that the Church can, in these times, serve as a basis for justice or the conservation of property, is simply absurd. Science not only does not sustain the doctrine of the Church, but is, in its development, entirely hostile to the Church. Art, formerly entirely devoted to the service of the Church, has wholly forsaken the Church. It is little to say that human life is now entirely emancipated from the Church; it has now, with regard to the Church, only contempt when the Church does not interfere with human affairs, and hatred when the Church seeks to re-assert its ancient privileges. The Church is still permitted a formal existence simply because men dread to shatter the chalice that once contained the water of life. In this way only can we account, in our age, for the existence of Catholicism, of Orthodoxy, and of the different Protestant churches.

All these churches Catholic, Orthodox, Protestant are like so many sentinels still keeping careful watch before the prison doors, although the prisoners have long been at liberty before their eyes, and even threaten their existence. All that actually constitutes life, that is, the activity of humanity towards progress and its own welfare, socialism, communism, the new politico-economical theories, utilitarianism, the liberty and equality of all social classes, and of men and women, all the moral principles of humanity, the sanctity of work, reason, science, art, all these that lend an impulse to the world's progress in hostility to the Church are only fragments of the doctrine which the Church has professed, and so carefully endeavored to conceal. In these times, the life of the world is entirely independent of the doctrine of the Church. The Church is left so far behind, that men no longer hear the voices of those who preach its doctrines. This is easily to be understood because the Church still clings to an organization of the world's life, which has been forsaken, and is rapidly falling to destruction.

Imagine a number of men rowing a boat, a pilot steering. The men rely upon the pilot, and the pilot steers well; but after a time the good pilot is replaced by another, who does not steer at all. The boat moves along rapidly and easily. At first the men do not notice the negligence of the new pilot; they are only pleased to find that the boat goes along so easily. Then they discover that the new pilot is utterly useless, and they mock at him, and drive him from his place.

The matter would not be so serious if the men, in thrusting aside the unskilful pilot, did not forget that without a pilot they are likely to take a wrong course. But so it is with our Christian society. The Church has lost its control; we move smoothly onward, and we are a long way from our point of departure. Science, that especial pride of this nineteenth century, is sometimes alarmed; but that is because of the absence of a pilot. We are moving onward, but to what goal? We organize our life without in the least knowing why, or to what end. But we can no longer be contented to live without knowing why, any more than we can navigate a boat without knowing the course that we are following.

If men could do nothing of themselves, if they were not responsible for their condition, they might very reasonably reply to the question, "Why are you in this situation?" "We do not know; but hero we are, and submit." But men are the builders of their own destiny, and more especially of the destiny of their children; and so when we ask, "Why do you bring together millions of troops, and why do you make soldiers of yourselves, and mangle and murder one another? Why have you expended, and why do you still expend, an enormous sum of human energy in the construction of useless and unhealthy cities? Why do you organize ridiculous tribunals, and send people whom you consider as criminals from France to Cayenne, from Russia to Siberia, from England to Australia, when you know the hopeless folly of it? Why do you abandon agriculture, which you love, for work in factories and mills, which you despise? Why do you bring up your children in a way that will force them to lead an existence which you find worthless? Why do you do this?" To all these questions men feel obliged to make some reply.

If this existence were an agreeable one, and men took pleasure in it, even then men would try to explain why they continued to live under such conditions. But all these things are terribly difficult; they are endured with murmuring and painful struggles, and men cannot refrain from reflecting upon the motive which impels them to such a course. They must cease to maintain the accepted organization of existence, or they must explain why they give it their support. And so men never have allowed this question to pass unanswered. We find in all ages some attempt at a response. The Jew lived as he lived, that is, made war, put criminals to death, built the Temple, organized his entire existence in one way and not another, because, as he was convinced, he thereby followed the laws which God him self had promulgated. We may say the same of the Hindu, the Chinaman, the Roman, and the Mohammedan. A similar response was given by the Christian a century ago, and is given by the great mass of Christians now.

A century ago, and among the ignorant now, the nominal Christian makes this reply: "Compulsory military service, wars, tribunals, and the death penalty, all exist in obedience to the law of God transmitted to us by the Church. This is a fallen world. All the evil that exists, exists by God's will, as a punishment for the sins of men. For this reason we can do nothing to palliate evil. "We can only save our own souls by faith, by the sacraments, by prayers, and by submission to the will of God as transmitted by the Church. The Church teaches us that all Christians should unhesitatingly obey their rulers, who are the Lord's anointed, and obey also persons placed in authority by rulers; that they ought to defend their property and that of others by force, wage war, inflict the death penalty, and in all things submit to the authorities, who command by the will of God."

Whatever we may think of the reasonableness of these explanations, they once sufficed for a believing Christian, as similar explanations satisfied a Jew or a Mohammedan, and men were not obliged to renounce all reason for living according to a law which they recognized as divine. But in this time only the most ignorant people have faith in any such explanations, and the number of these diminishes every day and every hour. It is impossible to check this tendency. Men irresistibly follow those who lead the way, and sooner or later must pass over the same ground as the advance guard. The advance guard is now in a critical position; those who compose it organize life to suit themselves, prepare the same conditions for those who are to follow, and absolutely have not the slightest idea of why they do so. No civilized man in the vanguard of progress is able to give any reply now to the direct questions, why do you lead the life that you do lead? Why do you establish the conditions that you do establish?" I have propounded these questions to hundreds of people, and never have got from them a direct reply. Instead of a direct reply to the direct question, I have received in return a response to a question that I had not asked.

When we ask a Catholic, or Protestant, or Orthodox believer why he leads an existence contrary to the doctrine of Jesus, instead of making a direct response he begins to speak of the melancholy state of scepticism characteristic of this generation, of evil-minded persons who spread doubt broadcast among the masses, of the importance of the future of the existing Church. But he will not tell you why he does not act in conformity to the commands of the religion that he professes. Instead of speaking of his own condition, he will talk to you about the condition of humanity in general, and of that of the Church, as if his own life were not of the slightest significance, and his sole preoccupations were the salvation of humanity, and of what he calls the Church.

A philosopher of whatever school he may be, whether an idealist or a spiritualist, a pessimist or a positivist, if we ask of him why he lives as he lives, that is to say, in disaccord with his philosophical doctrine, will begin at once to talk about the progress of humanity and about the historical law of this progress which he has discovered, and in virtue of which humanity gravitates toward righteousness. But he never will make any direct reply to the question why he himself, on his own account, does not live in harmony with what he recognizes as the dictates of reason. It would seem as if the philosopher were as preoccupied as the believer, not with his personal life, but with observing the effect of general laws upon the development of humanity.

The "average" man (that is, one of the immense majority of civilized people who are half sceptics and half believers, and who all, without exception, deplore existence, condemn its organization, and predict universal destruction), the average man, when we ask him why he continues to lead a life that he condemns, without making any effort towards its amelioration, makes no direct reply, but begins at once to talk about things in general, about justice, about the State, about commerce, about civilization.

If he be a member of the police or a prosecuting attorney, he asks, "And what would become of the State, if I, to ameliorate my existence, were to cease to serve it?" "What would become of commerce?" is his demand if he be a merchant; "What of civilization, if I cease to work for it, and seek only to better my own condition?" will be the objection of another. His response always will be in this form, as if the duty of his life were not to seek the good conformable to his nature, but to serve the State, or commerce, or civilization.

The average man replies in just the same manner, as does the believer or the philosopher. Instead of making the question a personal one, he glides at once to generalities. This subterfuge is employed simply because the believer and the philosopher, and the average man have no positive doctrine concerning existence, and cannot, therefore, reply to the personal question, "What of your own life?" They are disgusted and humiliated at not possessing the slightest trace of a doctrine with regard to life, for no one can live in peace without some understanding of what life really means. But nowadays only Christians cling to a fantastic and worn-out creed as an explanation of why life is as it is, and is not otherwise. Only Christians give the name of religion to a system which is not of the least use to anyone. Only among Christians is life separated from any or all doctrine, and left without any definition whatever. Moreover, science, like tradition, has formulated from the fortuitous and abnormal condition of humanity a general law.

Learned men, such as Tiele and Spencer, treat religion as a serious matter, understanding by religion the metaphysical doctrine of the universal principle, without suspecting that they have lost sight of religion as a whole by confining their attention entirely to one of its phases.

From all this we get very extraordinary results. We see learned and intelligent men artlessly believing that they are emancipated from all religion simply because they reject the metaphysical explanation of the universal principle which satisfied a former generation. It does not occur to them that men cannot live without some theory of existence; that every human being lives according to some principle, and that this principle by which he governs his life is his religion. The people of whom we have been speaking are persuaded that they have reasonable convictions, but that they have no religion. Nevertheless, however serious their asseverations, they have a religion from the moment that they undertake to govern their actions by reason, for a reasonable act is determined by some sort of faith. Now their faith is in what they are told to do. The faith of those who deny religion is in a religion of obedience to the will of the ruling majority; in a word, submission to established authority.

We may live a purely animal life according to the doctrine of the world, without recognizing any con trolling motive more binding than the rules of established authority, but he who lives this way cannot affirm that he lives a reasonable life. Before affirming that we live a reasonable life, we must determine what is the doctrine of the life which we regard as reasonable. Alas! Wretched men that we are, we possess not the semblance of any such doctrine, and more than that, we have lost all perception of the necessity for a reasonable doctrine of life.

Ask the believers or sceptics of this age, what doctrine of life they follow. They will be obliged to confess that they follow but one doctrine, the doctrine based upon laws formulated by the judiciary or by legislative assemblies, and enforced by the police the favorite doctrine of most Europeans. They know that this doctrine does not come from on high, or from prophets, or from sages; they are continually finding fault with the laws drawn up by the judiciary or formulated by legislative assemblies, but nevertheless they submit to the police charged with their enforcement. They submit without murmuring to the most terrible exactions. The clerks employed by the judiciary or the legislative assemblies decree by statute that every young man must be ready to take up arms, to kill others, and to die himself, and that all parents who have adult sons must favor obedience to this law which was drawn up yesterday by a mercenary official, and may be revoked tomorrow.

We have lost sight of the idea that a law may be in itself reasonable, and binding upon every one in spirit as well as in letter. The Hebrews possessed a law which regulated life, not by forced obedience to its requirements, but by appealing to the conscience of each individual; and the existence of this law is considered as an exceptional attribute of the Hebrew people. That the Hebrews should have been willing to obey only what they recognized by spiritual perception as the incontestable truth direct from God is considered a remarkable national trait. But it appears that the natural and normal state of civilized men is to obey what to their own knowledge is decreed by despicable officials and enforced by the cooperation of armed police.

The distinctive trait of civilized man is to obey what the majority of men regard as iniquitous, contrary to conscience. I seek in vain in civilized society as it exists today for any clearly formulated moral bases of life. There are none. No perception of their necessity exists. On the contrary, we find the extraordinary conviction that they are superfluous; that religion is nothing more than a few words about God and a future life, and a few ceremonies very useful for the salvation of the soul according to some, and good for nothing according to others; but that life happens of itself and has no need of any fundamental rule, and that we have only to do what we are told to do.

The two substantial sources of faith, the doctrine that governs life, and the explanation of the meaning of life, are regarded as of very unequal value. The first is considered as of very little importance, and as having no relation to faith whatever; the second, as the explanation of a bygone state of existence, or as made up of speculations concerning the historical development of life, is considered as of great significance. As to all that constitutes the life of man expressed in action, the members of our modern society depend willingly for guidance upon people who, like themselves, know not why they direct their fellows to live in one way and not in another. This disposition holds good whether the question at issue is to decide whether to kill or not to kill, to judge or not to judge, to bring up children in this way or in that. And men look upon an existence like this as reasonable, and have no feeling of shame!

The explanations of the Church which pass for faith, and the true faith of our generation, which is in obedience to social laws and the laws of the State, have reached a stage of sharp antagonism. The majority of civilized people have nothing to regulate life but faith in the police. This condition would be unbearable if it were universal. Fortunately there is a remnant, made up of the noblest minds of the age, who are not contented with this religion, but have an entirely different faith with regard to what the life of man ought to be. These men are looked upon as the most malevolent, the most dangerous, and generally as the most unbelieving of all human beings, and yet they are the only men of our time believing in the Gospel doctrine, if not as a whole, at least in part. These people, as a general thing, know little of the doctrine of Jesus; they do not understand it, and, like their adversaries, they refuse to accept the leading principle of the religion of Jesus, which is to resist not evil; often they have noth-ing but a hatred for the name of Jesus; but their whole faith with regard to what life ought to be is unconsciously based upon the humane and eternal truths comprised in the Christian doctrine. This remnant, in spite of calumny and persecution, are the only ones who do not tamely submit to the orders of the first comer. Consequently they are the only ones in these days who live a rea-sonable and not an animal life, the only ones who have faith.

The connecting link between the world and the Church, al-though carefully cherished by the Church, becomes more and more attenuated. Today it is little more than a hindrance. The union between the Church and the world has no longer any jus-tification. The mysterious process of maturation is going on be-fore our eyes. The connecting bond will soon be severed, and the vital social organism will begin to exercise its functions as a wholly independent existence. The doctrine of the Church, with its dogmas, its councils, and its hierarchy, is manifestly united to the doctrine of Jesus. The connecting link is as perceptible as the cord which binds the newborn child to its mother; but as the umbilical cord and the placenta become after parturition useless pieces of flesh, which are carefully buried out of regard for what they once nourished, so the Church has become a useless or-ganism, to be preserved, if at all, in some museum of curiosities out of regard for what it has once been. As soon as respiration and circulation are established, the former source of nutrition becomes a hindrance to life. Vain and foolish would it be to at-tempt to retain the bond, and to force the child that has come into the light of day to receive its nourishment by a pre-natal process. But the deliverance of the child from the maternal tie does not ensure life. The life of the newly born depends upon another bond of union which is established between it and its mother that its nourishment may be maintained.

And so it must be with our Christian world of today. The doc-trine of Jesus has brought the world into the light. The Church, one of the organs of the doctrine of Jesus, has fulfilled its mission and is now useless. The world cannot be bound to the Church; but the deliverance of the world from the Church will not ensure life. Life will begin when the world perceives its own weakness and the necessity for a different source of strength. The Christian world feels this necessity: it proclaims its helplessness, it feels the impossibility of depending upon its former means of nourishment, the inadequacy of any other form of nourishment except that of the doctrine by which it was brought forth. This modern European world of ours, apparently so sure of itself, so bold, so decided, and within so preyed upon by terror and despair, is exactly in the situation of a newly born animal: it writhes, it cries aloud, it is perplexed, it knows not what to do; it feels that its former source of nourishment is withdrawn, but it knows not where to seek for another. A newly born lamb shakes its head, opens its eyes and looks about, and leaps, and bounds, and would make us think by its apparently intelligent movements that it already has mastered the secret of living; but of this the "poor little creature knows nothing. The impetuosity and energy it displays were drawn from its mother through a medium of transmission that has just been broken, nevermore to be renewed. The situation of the new comer is one of delight, and at the same time is full of peril. It is animated by youth and strength, but it is lost if it cannot avail itself of the nourishment only to be had from its mother.

And so it is with our European world. What complex activities, what energy, what intelligence, does it apparently possess! It would seem as if all its deeds were governed by reason. With what enthusiasm, what vigor, what youthfulness do the denizens of this modern world manifest their abounding vitality! The arts and sciences, the various industries, political and administrative de tails, all are full of life. But this life is due to inspiration received through the connecting link that binds it to its source. The Church, by transmitting the truth of the doctrine of Jesus, has communicated life to the world. Upon this nourishment the world has grown and developed. But the Church has had its day and is now superfluous.

The world is possessed of a living organism; the moans by which it formerly received its nourishment has withered away, and it has not yet found another; and it seeks everywhere, everywhere but at the true source of life. It still possesses the animation derived from nourishment already received, and it does not yet understand that its future nourishment is only to be had from one source, and by its own efforts. The world must now understand that the period of gestation is ended, and that a new process of conscious nutrition must henceforth maintain its life. The truth of the doctrine of Jesus, once unconsciously absorbed by humanity through the organism of the Church, must now be consciously recognized; for in the truth of this doctrine humanity has always obtained its vital force. Men must lift up the torch of truth, which has so long remained concealed, and carry it before them, guiding their actions by its light.

The doctrine of Jesus, as a religion that governs the actions of men and explains to them the meaning of life, is now before the world just as it was eighteen hundred years ago. Formerly the world had the explanations of the Church which, in concealing the doctrine, seemed in itself to offer a satisfactory interpretation of life; but now the time is come when the Church has lost its usefulness, and the world, having no other means for sustaining its true existence, can only feel its helplessness and go for aid directly to the doctrine of Jesus.

Now, Jesus first taught men to believe in the light, and that the light is within themselves. Jesus taught men to lift on high the light of reason. He taught them to live, guiding their actions by thin light, and to do nothing contrary to reason. It is unreasonable, it is foolish, to go out to kill Turks or Germans; it is unreasonable to make use of the labor of others that you and yours may be clothed in the height of fashion and maintain that mortal source of ennui, a salon; it is unreasonable to take people already corrupted by idleness and depravity and shut them up within prison walls, and thereby devote them to an existence of absolute idleness and depravation; it is unreasonable to live in the pestilential air of cities when a purer atmosphere is within your reach; it is unreasonable to base the education of your children on the grammatical laws of dead languages; all this is unreasonable, and yet it is today the life of the European world, which lives a life of no meaning; which acts, but acts without a purpose, having no confidence in reason, and existing in opposition to its decrees.

The doctrine of Jesus is the light. The light shines forth, and the darkness cannot conceal it. Men cannot deny it; men cannot refuse to accept its guidance. They must depend on the doctrine of Jesus, which penetrates among all the errors with which the life of men is surrounded. Like the in sensible ether filling universal space, enveloping all created things, so the doctrine of Jesus is inevitable for every man in whatever situation he may be found. Men cannot refuse to recognize the doctrine of Jesus; they may deny the metaphysical explanation of life which it gives (we may deny everything), but the doctrine of Jesus alone offers rules for the conduct of life without which humanity has never lived, and never will be able to live; without which no human being has lived or can live, if he would live as man should live, a reasonable life. The power of the doctrine of Jesus is not in its explanation of the meaning of life, but in the rules that it gives for the conduct of life. The metaphysical doctrine of Jesus is not new; it is that eternal doctrine of humanity inscribed in all the hearts of men, and preached by all the prophets of all the ages. The power of the doctrine of Jesus is in the application of this metaphysical doctrine to life.

The metaphysical basis of the ancient doctrine of the Hebrews, which enjoined love to God and men, is identical with the metaphysical basis of the doctrine of Jesus. But the application of this doctrine to life, as expounded by Moses, was very different from the teachings of Jesus. The Hebrews, in applying the Mosaic law to life, were obliged to fulfil six hundred and thirteen commandments, many of which were absurd and cruel, and yet all were based upon the authority of the Scriptures. The doctrine of life, as given by Jesus upon the same metaphysical basis, is expressed in five reasonable and beneficent commandments, having an obvious and justifiable meaning, and embracing within their restrictions the whole of human life. A Jew, a disciple of Confucius, a Buddhist, or a Mohammedan, who sincerely doubts the truth of his own religion, cannot refuse to accept the doctrine of Jesus; much less, then, can this doctrine be rejected by the Christian world of today, which is now living without any moral law. The doctrine of Jesus cannot interfere in any way with the manner in which men of today regard the world; it is, to begin with, in harmony with their metaphysics, but it gives them what they have not now, what is indispensable to their existence, and what they all seek, it offers them a way of life; not an unknown way, but a way already explored and familiar to all.

Let us suppose that you are a sincere Christian; it matters not of what confession. You believe in the creation of the world, in the Trinity, in the fall and redemption of man, in the sacraments, in prayer, in the Church. The doctrine of Jesus is not opposed to your dogmatic belief, and is absolutely in harmony with your theory of the origin of the universe; and it offers you something that you do not possess. While you retain your present religion you feel that your own life and the life of the world is full of evil that you know not how to remedy. The doctrine of Jesus (which should be binding upon you since it is the doctrine of your own God) offers you simple and practical rules which will surely deliver you, you and your fellows, from the evils with which you are tormented.

Believe, if you will, in paradise, in hell, in the pope, in the Church, in the sacraments, in the redemption; pray according to the dictates of your faith, attend upon your devotions, sing your hymns, but all this will not prevent you from practising the five commandments given by Jesus for your welfare: Be not angry; Do not commit adultery; Take no oaths; Resist not evil; Do not make war. It may happen that you will break one of these rules; you will perhaps yield to temptation, and violate one of them, just as you violate the rules of your present religion, or the articles of the civil code, or the laws of custom. In the same way you may, perhaps, in moments of temptation, fail of observing all the commandments of Jesus. But, in that case, do not calmly sit down as you do now, and so organize your existence as to render it a task of extreme difficulty not to be angry, not to commit adultery, not to take oaths, not to resist evil, not to make war; organize rather an existence which shall render the doing of all these things as difficult as the non-performance of them is now laborious. You cannot refuse to recognize the validity of these rules, for they are the commandments of the God whom you pretend to worship.

Let us suppose that you are an unbeliever, a philosopher; it matters not of what special school. You affirm that the progress of the world is in accordance with a law that you have discovered. The doctrine of Jesus does not oppose your views; it is in harmony with the law that you have discovered. But, aside from this law, in pursuance of which the world will in the course of a thousand years reach a state of felicity, there is still your own personal life to be considered. This life you can use by living in conformity to reason, or you can waste it by living in opposition to reason, and you have now for its guidance no rule whatever, except the decrees drawn up by men whom you do not esteem, and enforced by the police. The doctrine of Jesus offers you rules which are assuredly in accord with your law of "altruism," which is nothing but a feeble paraphrase of this same doctrine of Jesus.

Let us suppose that you are an average man, half sceptic, half believer, one who has no time to analyze the meaning of human life, and one therefore who has no determinate theory of existence. You live as lives the rest of the world about you. The doctrine of Jesus is not at all contrary to your condition. You are incapable of reason, of verifying the truths of the doctrines that are taught you; it is easier for you to do as others do. But however modest may be your estimate of your powers of reason, you know that you have within you a judge that sometimes approves your acts and sometimes condemns them. However modest your social position, there are occasions when you are bound to reflect and ask your self, "Shall I follow the example of the rest of the world, or shall I act in accordance with my own judgment?" It is precisely on these occasions when you are called upon to solve some problem with regard to the conduct of life, that the commandments of Jesus appeal to you in all their efficiency. The commandments of Jesus will surely respond to your inquiry, because they apply to your whole existence. The response will be in accord with your reason and your conscience. If you are nearer to faith than to unbelief, you will, in following these commandments, act in harmony with the will of God. If you are nearer to scepticism than to belief, you will, in following the doctrine of Jesus, govern your actions by the laws of reason, for the commandments of Jesus make manifest their own meaning, and their own justification.

"Now is the judgment of this world: now shall the prince of this world be cast out." (John xii. 31.)

"These things have I spoken unto you, that in me ye may have peace. In the world ye have tribulation: but be of good cheer; I have overcome the world." (John xvi. 33.)

The world, that is, the evil in the world, is overcome. If evil still exists in the world, it exists only through the influence of inertia; it no longer contains the principle of vitality. For those who have faith in the commandments of Jesus, it does not exist at all. It is vanquished by an awakened conscience, by the elevation of the son of man. A train that has been put in motion continues to move in the direction in which it was started; but the time comes when the intelligent effort of a controlling hand is made manifest, and the movement is reversed.

"Ye are of God, and have overcome them because greater is he that is within you than he that is in the world." (1 John v. 4.)

The faith that triumphs over the doctrines of the world is faith in the doctrine of Jesus.

Chapter 12

I BELIEVE IN THE DOCTRINE of Jesus, and this is my religion:

I believe that nothing but the fulfilment of the doctrine of Jesus can give true happiness to men. I believe that the fulfilment of this doctrine is possible, easy, and pleasant. I believe that although none other follows this doctrine, and I alone am left to practise it, I cannot refuse to obey it, if I would save my life from the certainty of eternal loss; just as a man in a burning house if he find a door of safety, must go out, so I must avail myself of the way to salvation. I believe that my life according to the doctrine of the world has been a torment, and that a life according to the doctrine of Jesus can alone give me in this world the happiness for which I was destined by the Father of Life. I believe that this doctrine is essential to the welfare of humanity, will save me from the certainty of eternal loss, and will give me in this world the greatest possible sum of happiness. Believing thus, I am obliged to practise its commandments.

"The law was given by Moses; grace and truth came by Jesus Christ." (John i. 17.)

The doctrine of Jesus is a doctrine of grace and truth. Once I knew not grace and knew not truth. Mistaking evil for good, I fell into evil, and I doubted the righteousness of my tendency toward good. I understand and believe now that the good toward which I was attracted is the will of the Father, the essence of life.

Jesus has told us to live in pursuit of the good, and to beware of snares and temptations σκανδαλος which, by enticing us with the semblance of good, draw us away from true goodness, and lead us into evil. He has taught us that our welfare is to be sought in fellowship with all men; that evil is a violation of fellowship with the son of man, and that we must not deprive ourselves of the welfare to be had by obedience to his doctrine.

Jesus has demonstrated that fellowship with the son of man, the love of men for one another, is not merely an ideal after which men are to strive; he has shown us that this love and this fellowship are natural attributes of men in their normal condition, the condition into which children are born, the condition in which all men would live if they were not drawn aside by error, illusions, and temptations.

In his commandments, Jesus has enumerated clearly and unmistakably the temptations that interfere with this natural condition of love and fellow ship and render it a prey to evil. The commandments of Jesus offer the remedies by which I must save myself from the temptations that have deprived me of happiness; and so I am forced to believe that these commandments are true. Happiness was within my grasp and I destroyed it. In his commandments Jesus has shown me the temptations that lead to the destruction of happiness. I can no longer work for the destruction of my happiness, and in this determination, and in this alone, is the substance of my religion.

Jesus has shown me that the first temptation destructive of happiness is enmity toward men, anger against them. I cannot refuse to believe this, and so I cannot willingly remain at enmity with others. I cannot, as I could once, foster anger, be proud of it, fan it into flame, justify it, regarding myself as an intelligent and superior man and others as useless and foolish people. Now, when I give up to anger, I can only realize that I alone am guilty, and seek to make peace with those who have aught against me.

But this is not all. While I now see that anger is an abnormal, pernicious, and morbid state, I also perceive the temptation that led me into it. The temptation was in separating myself from my fellows, recognizing only a few of them as my equals, and regarding all the others as persons of no account (*rekim*) or as uncultivated animals (fools). I see now that this wilful separation from other men, this judgment of Raca or fool passed upon others, was the principal source of my disagreements. In looking over my past life I saw that I had rarely permitted my auger to rise against those whom I considered as my equals, whom I seldom abused. But the least disagreeable action on the part of one whom I considered an inferior inflamed my anger and led me to abusive words or actions, and the more superior I felt myself to be, the less careful I was of my temper; sometimes the mere supposition that a man was of a lower social position than myself was enough to provoke me to an outrageous manner.

I understand now that he alone is above others who is humble with others and makes himself the servant of all. I understand now why those that are exalted in the sight of men are an abomination to God, who has declared woe upon the rich and mighty and invoked blessedness upon the poor and humble. Now I understand this truth, I have faith in it, and this faith has transformed my perception of what is right and important, and what is wrong and despicable. Everything that once seemed to me right and important, such as honors, glory, civilization, wealth, the complications and refinements of existence, luxury, rich food, fine clothing, etiquette, have become for me wrong and despicable. Everything that formerly seemed to me wrong and despicable, such as rusticity, obscurity, poverty, austerity, simplicity of surroundings, of food, of clothing, of manners, all have now become right and important to me. And so although I may at times give myself up to anger and abuse another, I cannot deliberately yield to wrath and so deprive myself of the true source of happiness, fellowship and love; for it is possible that a man should lay a snare for his own feet and so be lost. Now, I can no longer give my support to anything that lifts me above or separates me from others. I cannot, as I once did, recognize in myself or others titles or ranks or qualities aside from the title and quality of manhood. I can no longer seek for fame and glory; I can no longer cultivate a system of instruction which separates me from men. I cannot in my surroundings, my food, my clothing, my manners, strive for what not only separates me from others but renders me a reproach to the majority of mankind.

Jesus showed me another temptation destructive of happiness, that is, debauchery, the desire to possess another woman than her to whom I am united. I can no longer, as I did once, consider my sensuality as a sublime trait of human nature. I can no longer justify it by my love for the beautiful, or my amorousness, or the faults of my companion. At the first inclination toward debauchery I cannot fail to recognize that I am in a morbid and abnormal state, and to seek to rid myself of the besetting sin.

Knowing that debauchery is an evil, I also know its cause, and can thus evade it. I know now that the principal cause of this temptation is not the necessity for the sexual relation, but the abandonment of wives by their husbands, and of husbands by their wives. I know now that a man who forsakes a woman, or a woman who forsakes a man, when the two have once been united, is guilty of the divorce which Jesus forbade, because men and women abandoned by their first companions are the original cause of all the debauchery in the world.

In seeking to discover the influences that led to debauchery, I found one to be a barbarous physical and intellectual education that developed the erotic passion which the world endeavors to justify by the most subtile arguments. But the principal influence I found to be the abandonment of the woman to whom I had first been united, and the situation of the abandoned women around me. The principal source of temptation was not in carnal desires, but in the fact that those desires were not satisfied in the men and women by whom I was surrounded. I now understand the words of Jesus when he says:

"He which made them from the beginning, made them male and female . . . . So that they are no more twain, but one flesh. What, therefore, God hath joined together, let not man put asunder." (Matt, vi. 4–6.)

I understand now that monogamy is the natural law of humanity, which cannot with impunity be violated. I now understand perfectly the words declaring that the man or woman who separates from a companion to seek another, forces the forsaken one to resort to debauchery, and thus introduces into the world an evil that returns upon those who cause it.

This I believe; and the faith I now have has transformed my opinions with regard to the right and important, and the wrong and despicable, things of life. What once seemed to me the most delightful existence in the world, an existence made up of dainty, aesthetic pleasures and passions, is now revolting to me.

And a life of simplicity and indigence, which moderates the sexual desires, now seems to me good. The human institution of marriage, which gives a nominal sanction to the union of man and woman, I regard as of less grave importance than that the union, when accomplished, should be regarded as the will of God, and never be broken.

Now, when in moments of weakness I yield to the promptings

of desire, I know the snare that would deliver me into evil, and so I cannot deliberately plan my method of existence as formerly I was accustomed to do. I no longer habitually cherish physical sloth and luxury, which excite to excessive sensuality. I can no longer pursue amusements which are oil to the fire of amorous sensuality, the reading of romances and the most of poetry, listening to music, attendance at theatres and balls, amusements that once seemed to me elevated and refining, but which I now see to be injurious. I can no longer abandon the woman with whom I have been united, for I know that by forsaking her, I set a snare for myself, for her, and for others. I can no longer encourage the gross and idle existence of others. I can no longer encourage or take part in licentious pastimes, romantic literature, plays, operas, balls, which are so many snares for myself and for others. I cannot favor the celibacy of persons fitted for the marriage relation. I cannot encourage the separation of wives from their husbands. I cannot make any distinction between unions that are called by the name of marriage, and those that are denied this name. I am obliged to consider as sacred and absolute the sole and unique union by which man is once for all indissolubly bound to the first woman with whom he has been united.

Jesus has shown me that the third temptation destructive to true happiness is the oath. I am obliged to believe his words; consequently, I cannot, as I once did, bind myself by oath to serve anyone for any purpose, and I can no longer, as I did formerly, justify myself for having taken an oath because "it would harm no one," because everybody did the same, because it is necessary for the State, because the consequences might be bad for me or for someone else if I refuse to submit to this exaction. I know now that it is an evil for myself and for others, and I cannot conform to it.

Nor is this all. I now know the snare that led me into evil, and I can no longer act as an accomplice. I know that the snare is in the use of God's name to sanction an imposture, and that the imposture consists in promising in advance to obey the commands of one man, or of many men, while I ought to obey the commands of God alone. I know now that evils the most terrible of all in their result war, imprisonments, capital punishment exist only because of the oath, in virtue of which men make themselves instruments of evil, and believe that they free them selves from all responsibility. As I think now of the many evils that have impelled me to hostility and hatred, I see that they all originated with the oath, the engagement to submit to the will of others. I understand now the meaning of the words:

"But let your speech be, Yea, yea; nay, nay; and whatsoever is more than these is of evil." (Matt. v. 37.)

Understanding this, I am convinced that the oath is destructive of my true welfare and of that of others, and this belief changes my estimate of right and wrong, of the important and despicable. What once seemed to me right and important, the promise of fidelity to the government supported by the oath, the exacting of oaths from others, and all acts contrary to conscience, done because of the oath, now seem to me wrong and despicable. Therefore I can no longer evade the commandment of Jesus forbidding the oath, I can no longer bind myself by oath to anyone, I cannot exact an oath from another, I cannot encourage men to take an oath, or to cause others to take an oath; nor can I regard the oath as necessary, important, or even inoffensive.

Jesus has shown me that the fourth temptation destructive to my happiness is the resort to violence for the resistance of evil. I am obliged to believe that this is an evil for myself and for others; consequently, I cannot, as I did once, deliberately resort to violence, and seek to justify my action with the pretext that it is indispensable for the defence of my person and property, or of the persons and property of others. I can no longer yield to the first impulse to resort to violence; I am obliged to renounce it, and to abstain from it altogether.

But this is not all. I understand now the snare that caused me to fall into this evil. I know now that the snare consisted in the erroneous belief that my life could be made secure by violence, by the defence of my person and property against the encroachments of others. I know now that a great portion of the evils that afflict mankind are due to this, that men, instead of giving their work for others, deprive themselves completely of the privilege of work, and forcibly appropriate the labor of their fellows. Every one regards a resort to violence as the best possible security for life and for property, and I now see that a great portion of the evil that I did myself, and saw others do, resulted from this practice. I understood now the meaning of the words:

"Not to be ministered unto, but to minister"

"The laborer is worthy of his food."

I believe now that my true welfare, and that of others, is possible only when I labor not for myself, but for another, and that I must not refuse to labor for another, but to give with joy that of which he has need. This faith has changed my estimate of what is right and important, and wrong and despicable. What once seemed to me right and important riches, proprietary rights, the point of honor, the maintenance of personal dignity and personal privileges have now become to me wrong and despicable. Labor for others, poverty, humility, the renunciation of property and of personal privileges, have become in my eyes right and important.

When, now, in a moment of forgetfulness, I yield to the impulse to resort to violence, for the defence of my person or property, or of the persons or property of others, I can no longer deliberately make use of this snare for my own destruction and the destruction of others. I can no longer acquire property. I can no longer resort to force in any form for my own defence or the defence of another. I can no longer co-operate with any power whose object is the defence of men and their property by violence. I can no longer act in a judicial capacity, or clothe myself with any authority, or take part in the exercise of any jurisdiction whatever. I can no longer encourage others in the support of tribunals, or in the exercise of authoritative administration.

Jesus has shown me that the fifth temptation that deprives me of well being, is the distinction that we make between compatriots and foreigners. I must believe this; consequently, if, in a moment of forgetfulness, I have a feeling of hostility toward a man of another nationality, I am obliged, in moments of reflection, to regard this feeling as wrong. I can no longer, as I did formerly, justify my hostility by the superiority of my own people over others, or by the ignorance, the cruelty, or the barbarism of another race. I can no longer refrain from striving to be even friendlier with a foreigner than with one of my own countrymen.

I know now that the distinction I once made between my own people and those of other countries is destructive of my welfare; but more than this,

I now know the snare that led me into this evil, and I can no longer, as I did once, walk deliberately and calmly into this snare. I know now that this snare consists in the erroneous belief that my welfare is dependent only upon the welfare of my countrymen, and not upon the welfare of all mankind. I know now that my fellowship with others cannot be shut off by a frontier, or by a government decree which decides that I belong to some particular political organization. I know now that all men are everywhere brothers and equals. When I think now of all the evil that I have done, that I have endured, and that I have seen about me, arising from national enmities, I see clearly that it is all due to that gross imposture called patriotism, love for one's native land. When I think now of my education, I see how these hateful feelings were grafted into my mind. I understand now the meaning of the words:

"Love your enemies, and pray for them that persecute you; that ye may be sons of your Father that is in heaven: for he maketh his sun to rise on the evil and the good, and sendeth rain on the just and the unjust"

I understand now that true welfare is possible for me only on condition that I recognize my fellowship with the whole world. I believe this, and the belief has changed my estimate of what is right and wrong, important and despicable. What once seemed to me right and important love of country, love for those of my own race, for the organization called the State, services rendered at the expense of the welfare of other men, military exploits now seem to me detestable and pitiable. What once seemed to me shameful and wrong renunciation of nationality, and the cultivation of cosmopolitanism now seem to me right and important. When, now, in a moment of forgetfulness, I sustain a Russian in preference to a foreigner, and desire the success of Russia or of the Russian people, I can no longer in lucid moments allow myself to be controlled by illusions so destructive to my welfare and the welfare of others. I can no longer recognize states or peoples; I can no longer take part in any difference between peoples or states, or any discussion between them either oral or written, much less in any service in behalf of any particular state. I can no longer cooperate with measures maintained by divisions between states, the collection of custom duties, taxes, the manufacture of arms and projectiles, or any act favoring armaments, military service, and, for a stronger reason, wars, neither can I encourage others to take any part in them.

I understand in what my true welfare consists, I have faith in that, and consequently I cannot do what would inevitably be destructive of that welfare. I not only have faith that I ought to live thus, but I have faith that if I live thus, and only thus, my life will attain its only possible meaning, and be reasonable, pleasant, and indestructible by death. I believe that my reasonable life, the light I bear with me, was given to me only that it might shine before men, not in words only, but in good deeds, that men may thereby glorify the Father. I believe that my life and my consciousness of truth is the talent confided to me for a good purpose, and that this talent fulfils its mission only when it is of use to others. I believe that I am a Ninevite with regard to other Jonahs from whom I have learned and shall learn of the truth; but that I am a Jonah in regard to other Ninevites to whom I am bound to transmit the truth. I believe that the only meaning of my life is to be attained by living in accordance with the light that is within me, and that I must allow this light to shine forth to be seen of all men. This faith gives me renewed strength to fulfil the doctrine of Jesus, and to overcome the obstacles which still arise in my pathway. All that once caused me to doubt the possibility of practising the doctrine of Jesus, everything that once turned me aside, the possibility of privations, and of suffering, and death, inflicted by those who know not the doctrine of Jesus, now confirm its truth and draw me into its service. Jesus said,

"When you have lifted up the son of Man, then shall you know that I am he" then shall you be drawn into my service, and I feel that I am irresistibly drawn to him by the influence of his doctrine. "The truth" he says again, "The truth shall make you free" and I know that I am in perfect liberty.

I once thought that if a foreign invasion occurred, or even if evil-minded persons attacked me, and I did not defend myself, I should be robbed and beaten and tortured and killed with those whom I felt bound to protect, and this possibility troubled me. But this that once troubled me now seems desirable and in conformity with the truth. I know now that the foreign enemy and the malefactors or brigands are all men like myself; that, like myself, they love good and hate evil; that they live as I live, on the borders of death; and that, with me, they seek for salvation, and will find it in the doctrine of Jesus. The evil that they do to me will be evil to them, and so can be nothing but good for me. But if truth is unknown to them, and they do evil thinking that they do good, I, who know the truth, am bound to reveal it to them, and this I can do only by refusing to participate in evil, and thereby confessing the truth by my example.

"But hither come the enemy, Germans, Turks, savages; if you do not make war on them, they will exterminate you!"

They will do nothing of the sort. If there were a society of Christian men that did evil to none and gave of their labor for the good of others, such a society would have no enemies to kill or to torture them. The foreigners would take only what the members of this society voluntarily gave, making no distinction between Russians, or Turks, or Germans. But when Christians live in the midst of a non-Christian society which defends itself by force of arm, and calls upon the Christians to join in waging war, then the Christians have an opportunity for revealing the truth to them who know it not. A Christian knowing the truth bears witness of the truth before others, and this testimony can be made manifest only by example. He must renounce war and do good to all men, whether they are foreigners or compatriots.

"But there are wicked men among compatriots; they will attack a Christian, and if the latter do not defend himself, will pillage and massacre him and his family." No; they will not do so. If all the members of this family are Christians, and consequently hold their lives only for the service of others, no man will be found insane enough to deprive such people of the necessaries of life or to kill them. The famous Maclay lived among the most bloodthirsty of savages; they did not kill him, they reverenced him and followed his teachings, simply because he did not fear them, exacted nothing from them, and treated them always with kindness.

"But what if a Christian lives in a non-Christian family, accustomed to defend itself and its property by a resort to violence, and is called upon to take part in measures of defence?" This solicitation is simply an appeal to the Christian to fulfil the decrees of truth. A Christian knows the truth only that he may show it to others, more especially to his neighbors and to those who are bound to him by ties of blood and friendship, and a Christian can show the truth only by refusing to join in the errors of others, by taking part neither with aggressors or defenders, but by abandoning all that he has to those who will take it from him, thus showing by his acts that he has need of nothing save the fulfilment of the will of God, and that he fears nothing except disobedience to that will.

"But how, if the government will not permit a member of the society over which it has sway, to refuse to recognize the fundamental principles of governmental order or to decline to fulfil the duties of a citizen? The government exacts from a Christian the oath, jury service, military service, and his refusal to conform to these demands may be punished by exile, imprisonment, and even by death." Then, once more, the exactions of those in authority are only an appeal to the Christian to manifest the truth that is in him. The exactions of those in authority are to a Christian the exactions of those who do not know the truth. Consequently, a Christian who knows the truth must bear witness of the truth to those who know it not. Exile and imprisonment and death afford to the Christian the possibility of bearing witness of the truth, not in words, but in acts. Violence, war, brigandage, executions, are not accomplished through the forces of unconscious nature; they are accomplished by men who are blinded, and do not know the truth. Consequently, the more evil these men do to Christians, the further they are from the truth, the more unhappy they are, and the more necessary it is that they should have knowledge of the truth. Now a Christian cannot make known his knowledge of truth except by abstaining from the errors that lead men into evil; he must render good for evil. This is the life work of a Christian, and if it is accomplished, death cannot harm him, for the meaning of his life can never be destroyed.

Men are united by error into a compact mass. The prevailing power of evil is the cohesive force that binds them together. The reasonable activity of humanity is to destroy the cohesive power of evil. Revolutions are attempts to shatter the power of evil by violence. Men think that by hammering upon the mass they will be able to break it in fragments, but they only make it more dense and impermeable than it was before. External violence is of no avail. The disruptive movement must come from within when molecule releases its hold upon molecule and the whole mass falls into disintegration. Error is the force that welds men together; truth alone can set them free. Now truth is truth only when it is in action, and then only can it be transmitted from man to man. Only truth in action, by introducing light into the conscience of each individual, can dissolve the homogeneity of error, and detach men one by one from its bonds.

This work has been going on for eighteen hundred years. It began when the commandments of Jesus were first given to humanity, and it will not cease till, as Jesus said, *"all things be accomplished"* (Matt. v. 18). The Church that sought to detach men from error and to weld them together again by the solemn affirmation that it alone was the truth, has long since fallen to decay. But the Church composed of men united, not by promises or sacraments, but by deeds of truth and love, has always lived and will live forever. Now, as eighteen hundred years ago, this Church is made up not of those who say "Lord, Lord," and bring forth iniquity, but of those who hear the words of truth and reveal them in their lives. The members of this Church know that life is to them a blessing as long as they maintain fraternity with others and dwell in the fellowship of the son of man; and that the blessing will be lost only to those who do not obey the commandments of Jesus. And so the members of this Church practise the commandments of Jesus and thereby teach them to others. Whether this Church be in numbers little or great, it is, nevertheless, the Church that shall never perish, the Church that shall finally unite within its bonds the hearts of all mankind.

"Fear not, little flock; for it is your Father's good purpose to give you the kingdom."

Appendix

WHEN COUNT TOLSTOY speaks of the Church and its dogmas, he refers especially, of course, to the Orthodox Greek Church, the national church of Russia. The following summary of the teachings of the Orthodox Greek Church is taken from Prof. T. M. Lindsay's article in the *Encyclopedia Britannica,* ninth edition, volume xi. p. 158. Variations from the Roman Catholic doctrine are indicated by small capitals, and variations from Protestant doctrine by italics. [Tr.]

Christianity is a divine revelation, communicated to mankind through Christ; its saving truths are to be learned from the Bible and tradition, the former having been written, and the latter maintained uncorrupted through the influence of the Holy Spirit; *the interpretation of the Bible belongs to the Church, which is taught by the Holy Spirit,* but every believer may read the Scriptures.

"According to the Christian revelation, God is a trinity, that is, the divine essence exists in three persons, perfectly equal in nature and dignity, the Father, the Son, and the Holy Ghost; The holy ghost proceeds from the father only. Besides the triune God, there is no other object of divine worship, but homage may be paid to the Virgin Mary, and reverence to the saints and to their pictures and relics.

"Man is born with a corrupt bias, which was not his at creation; the first man, when created, possessed Immortality, perfect wisdom, and a will regulated by reason. Through the first sin, Adam and his posterity lost Immortality, and his will received a bias towards evil. In this natural state, man, who, even before he actually sins, is a sinner before God by original or inherited sin, commits manifold actual transgressions; but he is not absolutely without power of will towards good, and is not always doing evil.

"Christ, the Son of God, became man in two natures, which internally and inseparably united make One Person, and, according to the eternal purpose of God, has obtained for man reconciliation with God and eternal life, inasmuch as he, by his vicarious death has made satisfaction to God for the world's sins; and this satisfaction was Perfectly commensurate with the sins of the world.

Man is made partaker of reconciliation in spiritual regeneration, which he attains to, being led and kept by the Holy Ghost. This divine help is offered to all men without distinction, and may be rejected. In order to attain to salvation, man is justified, and, when so justified, Can do no more than the commands of God. He may fall from this state of grace through mortal sin.

"Regeneration is offered by the word of God and in the sacraments, which, under visible signs, communicate God's invisible grace to Christians when administered *cum intentione.* There are seven mysteries or sacraments. Baptism entirely destroys original sin. In the Eucharist, the true body and blood of Christ are substantially present, and the elements are changed into the substance of Christ, whose body and blood are corporeally partaken of by communicants. All Christians should receive the bread and the Wine. The Eucharist is also an expiatory sacrifice. The new birth when lost may be restored through repentance, which is not merely (1) sincere sorrow, but also (2) confession of each individual sin to the priest, and (3) the discharge of penances imposed by the priest for the removal of the temporal punishment, which may have been imposed by God and the Church. Penance, accompanied by the judicial absolution of the priest, makes a true sacrament.

"The Church of Christ is the fellowship of All those who accept and profess all the articles of faith transmitted by the apostles, and approved by the general synods. Without this visible Church there is no salvation. It is under the abiding influence of the Holy Ghost, and therefore cannot err in matters of faith. Specially appointed persons are necessary in the service of the Church, and they form a threefold order, distinct jure divino from other Christians, of Bishops, Priests, and Deacons. The four patriarchs of equal dignity have the highest rank among the bishops, and the bishops united in a General Council represent the Church and infallibly decide, under the guidance of the Holy Ghost, all matters of faith and ecclesiastical life.

All ministers of Christ must be regularly called and appointed to their office, and are consecrated by the sacrament of orders. Bishops must be unmarried and Priests and deacons must not contract a second marriage. To all priests in common be longs, besides the preaching of the word, the administration Of the six sacraments, baptism, confirmation, penance, eucharist, matrimony, unction of the sick. The bishops alone can administer the sacrament of "Ecclesiastical ceremonies are part of the divine service; most of them have apostolic origin; and those connected with the sacrament must not be omitted by priests under pain of mortal sin."

Also available from White Crow Books

Marcus Aurelius—*The Meditations*
ISBN 978-1-907355-20-2

Elsa Barker—*Letters from a Living Dead Man*
ISBN 978-1-907355-83-7

Elsa Barker—*War Letters from the Living Dead Man*
ISBN 978-1-907355-85-1

Elsa Barker—*Last Letters from the Living Dead Man*
ISBN 978-1-907355-87-5

Richard Maurice Bucke—*Cosmic Consciousness*
ISBN 978-1-907355-10-3

G. K. Chesterton—*The Everlasting Man*
ISBN 978-1-907355-03-5

G. K. Chesterton—*Heretics*
ISBN 978-1-907355-02-8

G. K. Chesterton—*Orthodoxy*
ISBN 978-1-907355-01-1

Arthur Conan Doyle—*The Edge of the Unknown*
ISBN 978-1-907355-14-1

Arthur Conan Doyle—*The New Revelation*
ISBN 978-1-907355-12-7

Arthur Conan Doyle—*The Vital Message*
ISBN 978-1-907355-13-4

Arthur Conan Doyle with Simon Parke—*Conversations with Arthur Conan Doyle*
ISBN 978-1-907355-80-6

Leon Denis with Arthur Conan Doyle—*The Mystery of Joan of Arc*
ISBN 978-1-907355-17-2

The Earl of Dunraven—*Experiences in Spiritualism with D. D. Home*
ISBN 978-1-907355-93-6

Meister Eckhart with Simon Parke—*Conversations with Meister Eckhart*
ISBN 978-1-907355-18-9

Kahlil Gibran—*The Forerunner*
ISBN 978-1-907355-06-6

Kahlil Gibran—*The Madman*
ISBN 978-1-907355-05-9

Kahlil Gibran—*The Prophet*
ISBN 978-1-907355-04-2

Kahlil Gibran—*Sand and Foam*
ISBN 978-1-907355-07-3

Kahlil Gibran—*Jesus the Son of Man*
ISBN 978-1-907355-08-0

Kahlil Gibran—*Spiritual World*
ISBN 978-1-907355-09-7

Hermann Hesse—*Siddhartha*
ISBN 978-1-907355-31-8

D. D. Home—*Incidents
in my Life Part 1*
ISBN 978-1-907355-15-8

Mme. Dunglas Home; edited,
with an Introduction, by Sir
Arthur Conan Doyle—*D. D.
Home: His Life and Mission*
ISBN 978-1-907355-16-5

Andrew Lang—*The Book
of Dreams and Ghosts*
ISBN 978-1-907355-97-4

Edward C. Randall—
Frontiers of the Afterlife
ISBN 978-1-907355-30-1

Lucius Annaeus Seneca—*On Benefits*
ISBN 978-1-907355-19-6

Rebecca Ruter Springer—*Intra
Muros—My Dream of Heaven*
ISBN 978-1-907355-11-0

W. T. Stead—*After Death* or *Letters
from Julia: A Personal Narrative*
ISBN 978-1-907355-89-9

Leo Tolstoy, edited by Simon
Parke—*Tolstoy's Forbidden Words*
ISBN 978-1-907355-00-4

Leo Tolstoy—*A Confession*
ISBN 978-1-907355-24-0

Leo Tolstoy—*The Gospel in Brief*
ISBN 978-1-907355-22-6

Leo Tolstoy—*The Kingdom
of God is Within You*
ISBN 978-1-907355-27-1

Leo Tolstoy—*My Religion—
What I Believe*
ISBN 978-1-907355-23-3

Leo Tolstoy—*On Life*
ISBN 978-1-907355-91-2

Leo Tolstoy—*Twenty-three Tales*
ISBN 978-1-907355-29-5

Leo Tolstoy—*What is Religion
and other writings*
ISBN 978-1-907355-28-8

Leo Tolstoy—*Work While
Ye Have the Light*
ISBN 978-1-907355-26-4

Leo Tolstoy with Simon Parke—
Conversations with Tolstoy
ISBN 978-1-907355-25-7

Howard Williams with an
Introduction by Leo Tolstoy—*The
Ethics of Diet: An Anthology
of Vegetarian Thought*
ISBN 978-1-907355-21-9

**All titles available as eBooks, and select titles available in
Audiobook format from www.whitecrowbooks.com**

CPSIA information can be obtained at www.ICGtesting.com
Printed in the USA
BVOW02s0154050516

446721BV00001B/41/P